FAMILY CHRONICLE

FAMILY CHRONICLE

Vasco Pratolini

TRANSLATED
FROM THE ITALIAN
BY
MARTHA KING

ITALICA PRESS
NEW YORK
1988

Translation Copyright © 1988 by Martha King

Vasco Pratolini, *Cronaca familiare* Copyright © 1960
Arnoldo Mondadori Editore S.p.A., Milano

ITALICA PRESS, INC.
625 Main Street
New York, New York 10044

Library of Congress Cataloging-in-Publication Data

Pratolini, Vasco.
  Family chronicle.

  Translation of: Cronaca familiare.
  1. Pratolini, Vasco--Biography. 2. Authors,
Italian--20th century--Biography. I. Title.
  PQ4835.R37C6513 1988   853'.912 [B]   87-82245
  ISBN 0-934977-07-0 (pbk.)

Printed in the United States of America
5 4 3 2 1

Cover Art: Alexandra Eldridge

ABOUT THE TRANSLATOR

Martha King has lived in Tuscany since 1979. She received her Ph.D. degree in Italian from the University of Wisconsin and presently teaches Italian literature at the University of Maryland in Pisa. In addition to novels and short stories of Grazia Deledda, she has translated Maraini, Banti, Pasolini, Leopardi, Arcangeli and others.

INTRODUCTION

by

MARTHA KING

Although identity with a particular region in Italy is not central to the fiction of Vasco Pratolini in the same sense that Sicily, Sardinia and Rome are inseparable from the works of Verga, Deledda and Gadda, his hometown does play an important role.

Vasco Pratolini's fictional place is Florence, where he was born in 1913. And between the two world wars he grew up there in a workingman's section that stretches from behind Piazza Signoria to the church of Santa Croce. The elegance of Via Tornabuoni or Piazza Signoria is far from this area, though both are just around the corner. His streets have names like Via de' Magazzini, Via del Corno, Via del Parlascio.

In fact, Pratolini called one of his earliest published works *Via de' Magazzini* (1942) — a short street at right angles with the city hall, Palazzo Vecchio. There Pratolini lived as a small child. In this short novella he describes casts of shadow made by the stone buildings, the extremes of temperature in the shabby rented rooms, the sounds floating up from narrow, stone-paved streets — all as much a part of the drama of his poor childhood as his family and neighbors were. Constructing his fiction out of the material of his past, he describes his life with his grandparents while his father was away at war and recalls memories of his pregnant mother, who, because of her ill-health, was unable to buffer his solitary and isolated young life — the same cast of characters that appears in *Family Chronicle*. However, *Via de' Magazzini* illuminates some of the family history that is only, though most artfully, suggested by the brothers' conversations in *Family Chronicle*.

The description of his mother, for example: "Mama was dying from the baby that was to be born. I saw mama a few minutes during the day, in the morning and evening, to tell her good morning and good night. She was almost always sitting on her bed, with her long black hair spread out on the pillows that supported her."

One day his mother has "Valerio" sit on a rug beside her bed. "'Did they tell you that you are going to have a little brother? Will you love him?;' and since I didn't respond, she said: 'Don't love him. I don't want you to.' Between the mother and her child was created an absurd complicity that frightened the child."

That complicity recounted in *Via de' Magazzini* went further than a tacit agreement not to love his brother; he never wrote of him as a family character until Pratolini felt compelled to tell his story in *Family Chronicle*. The conspiratorial understanding of the mother and her small son in *Via de' Magazzini* would have a long-lasting effect, and perhaps it helps explain the author's need for the atonement he mentions in the preface.

Family Chronicle was written rapidly in 1945, in a pause between the writing of other longer novels. This story of the relationship of the novelist with his brother is the history of an affection that the author had to come to terms with, as he had come to terms with the death of his grandparents and mother, and with his father's new wife whom the boy could never allow to replace his mother. What had been previously left out of the author's novels and short stories had to be written.

By chance the younger brother grew up in an environment far from the dark narrow streets of Florence. The narrow suburban roads lined by stone walls in the hills far above Brunelleschi's dome and the tall clock tower of Palazzo Vecchio pass through vineyards and olive groves. Ferruccio, in Villa Rossa, lived a privileged, pampered life that could only earn the resentment and hate of the older, less-advantaged brother. *Family Chronicle* recounts the older brother's painful voyage from resentment to a sincere and forgiving recognition of weaknesses to a loving acceptance that, according to the preface to the reader, came too late.

Pratolini's detached, poetic treatment of an understandably emotional and personal subject raises this work to the level of fine narrative fiction. It belongs to a literary genre not readily classifiable, but *Family Chronicle* has nevertheless been critically and popularly recognized as one of the important Italian books of this century. The pages of this novel are suffused with a lyricism often wrenching in its command of the emotional instant. What begins as a description as banal as daily habit can end in an epiphany.

Biographical details are unnecessary to appreciate this novelist's work to its full; yet a few facts may help in understanding his position in Italian literature.

Pratolini went to live alone after he had trained as a typographer. At this time he was finally able to study and learn as he had long desired, and he set himself on a course of self-education that included the reading of Dante, Manzoni and Dickens, among others. His health deteriorated seriously, and he spent two years in several sanitariums for the cure of tuberculosis. On his return to Florence he began to write short pieces, concentrating on memories of his childhood in the proletarian environment there.

His acquaintance with the writer Elio Vittorini in Rome, author of the much acclaimed *Conversations in Sicily,* and with other intellectuals influenced both his literary and political ideas. Pratolini rejected the elitist and self-contained hermetic mode of writing then fashionable, for a realistic portrayal of the lower classes in provincial settings. This puts him in the same realistic camp as writers like Moravia, Gadda, Silone, and Verga before them. From a passive Fascist he became a socialist, a turn of conscience that led him to fight with the partisans in 1943-45.

In Florence from August 1938 to August 1939 Pratolini and the poet Alfonso Gatto jointly edited a magazine, *Campo di Marte,* whose avowed purpose was "to educate the people" about all the arts. From the first issue the *Dottrina Fascista* came under fire as being "out of phase with the real needs of our times;" and it could have been no surprise to the editors when the publication of their cultural magazine was suppressed.

Pratolini wrote other successful novels, set in Florence, such as *Il Quartiere, Le ragazze di San Frediano,* and *Metello,* each combining a lyrical tone with a particular social perspective — a n artistic melding of private and public history. But in no work of Pratolini's does the combination find such convincing and moving expression as in *Family Chronicle,* where Pratolini acknowledges the need to complete his fictional family, and in which, at the same time, he completes his own personal history.

"Memory bears witness to one's own myth," Pratolini wrote in an essay in the short-lived *Campo di Marte.* Perhaps in *Family Chronicle,* more than in any other work — through careful selection of past experience renewed in the present and transformed by art —Pratolini creates his own personal myth and in so doing creates an unforgettable experience for his readers.

Laiatico, Fall 1987

FAMILY CHRONICLE

Il fior de' tuoi gentili anni caduto.
Foscolo

TO THE READER

This book is not a work of the imagination. It is the author's conversation with his dead brother. In writing it the author was looking for consolation, nothing more. He has the remorse of having barely understood his brother's spirituality, and too late. These pages are therefore offered as an inadequate atonement.

Part One

1

When mama died you were twenty-five days old. By then you were far from her in the hills. The country people who took care of you gave you milk from a spotted cow; I even had some of it once when grandmother and I came to see you. It was thick and warm, a little bitter, bad tasting; it tasted so bad that I spit it out, spoiling my suit; grandmother gave me a slap. You liked that milk, were greedy for it, lapped it up. You were a nice fat baby, blond, with big blue eyes. "The picture of health," grandmother would tell the neighbors, drying her eyes forever wet with tears.

We came to see you in the hills almost every day, climbing up Costa de' Magnoli, Costa Scarpuccia. It was summer, July; every time we reached the top I wanted to stop to look at Saint George and the Dragon carved on the city gate, but grandmother would pull me along. White olive branches merged in the sun with other trees behind the stone walls lining Via San Leonardo. Beyond, the perfect plowed fields, gently sloping; a great chirping of cicadas and butterflies lost in the light. We never met anyone, a voice rarely came from the fields. The gates of the villas were always closed. I stamped my heels on purpose as I walked to make the echo louder. Between the walls and the street there was occasionally a grassy border where poppies grew. The tall doors of the farm houses stood half open, painted the same green as the big umbrellas the farmers used. A smell of milk and stables came from them.

In the house where you were staying the smell was in the rooms, absorbed by the walls. You would suck that milk from a bottle, puff out your cheeks, laugh. I was five years old and couldn't love you; everyone said mama died because of you.

One day we didn't find you at the house where they were taking care of you. They had taken you to visit the people at Villa Rossa who, attracted by your beauty, had become curious about your situation. Our wait for you to return was futile. The countrywoman said: "If they become fond of him it'll be a lucky thing, poor creature!"

2

Now to visit you at Villa Rossa meant preparing for a ceremony. Before ringing the bell of the service entrance grandmother would take a handkerchief from her bosom, wet it with saliva, and always find some mustache of dirt on my face. She wiped the dust from my shoes, made me blow my nose. The door opened magically. There was a small flight of stairs going up to the kitchen. The great silence of the villa would begin, a silence more intense than in the street — the chirping of the cicadas, the echo of footsteps, the buzzing of the large flies were extinguished there. Instinctively I walked on tip-toe. We went up the stairs; the deserted kitchen was always the same — the copper molds for baked foods glittered on the walls. Only the odor would change; there was a strong, agreeable smell of butter in the kitchen. The only thing alive was the tick-tock of the wall clock which emphasized the silence rather than breaking it.

Around the oilcloth-covered table we sat in white chairs, lifting them up so they wouldn't make any noise. If I rested my hands on the table grandmother would straighten me up with a look. At the end of the kitchen a door opened onto a corridor. We saw a mirrored coat rack where a jacket with gray and white stripes always hung; on the floor a red carpet. Above, a rectangular window let trees from a garden show through the curtains. You didn't go beyond that doorway until you could walk.

We would remain seated, immobile, as much as a quarter of an hour before a rustling would be heard from the corridor; grandmother would order me with her eyes to stand up, but she remained seated herself. Near the threshold the steps would stop; we would hear a barely perceptible tinkling of glassware, then the steps would go away. I would ask grandmother: "Who could that be?" Grandmother would put her finger to her lips, giving me a sharp look; through her closed lips a slight breath of air would escape: "Ssss...." Below the window hung a lithograph of wild game and fruit; I would look at it for a long time to amuse myself. Or I would stare at the clock to see the instant the minute hand moved.

We would be aware of a very silent footstep just in time to jump up from our chairs. In the doorway would appear a maid who smiled when she saw us, greet us with a nod, go to the icebox, open and close it (this took place behind my back); going out she would nod as she had when she entered. She also would tell us in a low voice: "He is coming soon. Make yourself comfortable."

Finally you would arrive in the arms of your new nurse who wore a cap. She was dressed in blue and wore a long white apron. She was a sturdy woman with a genial face; she was the only person whose compliments you found agreeable. You were always calm and peaceful, your eyes wide open, your hair very fine and short. You were fat and your upper lip protruded; you grasped the finger grand-mother held out to you. The nurse lowered you to my height and you smiled at me. Once when I started to touch your cheek you began to cry — you reacted as though I had pinched you. That day our visit was shorter than usual. Normally we would stay a quarter of an hour — the nurse would look at her watch; we always came between one meal and another.

At a certain moment your patron would arrive. He spoke in a bitter tone of voice, with a paternal inflection even toward grandmother. Although his hair was white, it nevertheless conferred a somewhat youthful energy to his dry, ivory-colored face. He made me uneasy. Sometimes his wife would also appear, her broad face framed by two bands of soft, voluminous, snow-white hair. Breathing harshly, she would immediately sit down. It was she who had discovered you at the farmer's house. She smiled by pressing her lips together.

I would return to my seat; everyone would make a circle around you. The nurse always stood, holding you in her arms while you waved your little hands and made everyone smile and commiserate over your fate, and made grandmother thank and bless your benefactors. Then the quarter of an hour would run out, and the nurse would say good-bye for you: "Say 'ciao' to grandmother, say 'ciao' to your little brother." We couldn't kiss you for hygienic reasons.

This took place once a week. It would also happen that while grandmother and I were waiting in the kitchen the maid would come to say that you were still sleeping and had to eat as soon as you woke up, then you had to take a walk in the garden, where we could not join you because the baron had visitors. She would send us away until the next week. Before we left she would offer us some toast with butter and marmalade. Orange marmalade.

3

The baron was a rich English gentleman, a Sir, who had grown old traveling over the world as a pastime, until he found the ideal residence in the hills of Florence. Your benefactor was his butler who had served him for forty years. His horizons were none other than those seen through the eyes of his master. At the end of the century, already at a ripe age, he had married the "head maid" who had given him two sons, now the house chauffeurs. He enjoyed indisputable authority; his power stopped just at the doorway of the gentleman's room. It was he who dressed the old baron, scrubbed his back in the bath, urged him to swallow the laxative. The servants both detested and admired him; he knew how to demonstrate the soundness of his reprimands to each one of them: to the cook he taught the correct recipe, to the gardener the reason for an unsuccessful grafting, to the laundress a better way to iron collars. And he knew the right moment to tell a joke and pat a maid on the bottom without diminishing his own prestige.

On those occasions, I imagine, his laugh would explode. But it isn't correct to call it a laugh. It was more like a sob, a wholly repressed hilarity expressed by shaking his body, blinking his eyes, showing his teeth, which were small, even, slightly opaque, like false teeth. He was moderate even in gaiety and, it could be said, fearful of disturbing the silence. That was the impression he gave — a man wrapped in silence. The silence in which the house was immersed. Normally he spoke in a low voice, with the clearly perceptible tone of a man who even in speaking had found the measure of silence. At that time I knew nothing more about him. Man-house-silence-laugh were all the associations I could make.

During our visits he would always laugh that way. He would make some motions with his hands in front of your eyes and you would respond by leaning your head to one side in the graceful gesture of babies. Then he would laugh. Grandmother and the nurse would also laugh. His face frightened me when he laughed like that. Sometimes he would come near me and put a finger under my chin to include me in the general fun. His finger was cold, even in the summer. He didn't inspire me to love him.

One night I dreamed that while laughing in that way he bent over your cradle and smothered you, killed you. I was in a corner of the room, behind the curtains, and didn't intervene even by shouting. I pawed the empty air and suddenly a hand met mine; I realized mama was by my side also silently assisting in the assassination. This dream was repeated periodically until I was nearly fifteen. Sometimes mama would let go of my hand and walk to your cradle; he would disappear immediately.

4

We came to see you on Thursdays. Grandmother had Thursday afternoon off from her part-time work and I was on vacation from school. Often on our return the wife of your patron would accompany us part of the way. She was now the linen maid and

Thursday was her free day. Months before, on one of her Thursday walks, she had stopped at the house of the people who were taking care of you. They furnished the milk to the villa and were eager to have her stop so they could show you off and tell her your story. The woman was touched; she said that when the baron wasn't there they could take you for a walk in the garden of the villa. She would be happy to see you again. Those country people minding you did not miss this opportunity, *for your own good,* they said. One day while their daughter was taking you out in the fresh air, she met the baron, between the hedges of boxwood and the flower beds, who had come back unexpectedly. In vain the butler signalled for her to disappear; perhaps the girl, "for your own good," and because of her vanity, didn't want "to disappear" among the paths or behind the greenhouse. Instead she went up to the old gentleman. The girl, I imagine, curtsied, just bending her knee; she showed him what she was holding. One should not surprise the baron with unexpected encounters. He asked the questions that kings ask in such dangerous situations, whether sincerely or merely politely is of little importance. He appeared to be touched by the story of that newborn orphaned from his mother and with his father in the hospital with war wounds. Turning to his butler he said condescendingly that the little one must be helped. You were a blond baby with blue eyes, you laughed with your gums showing, and waved your little hands.

Your destiny was now sealed. According to grandmother, mama was looking after you from paradise. Papa was also convinced of this, as were the neighbors, everyone. Only to grandfather did it

not seem a good thing. But grandfather died soon.
You never knew him.

5

I would think of you often, with irritation, with the
same feeling that a boy of six remembers something
bad that happened, with a sense of irreparable
guilt. It almost made me cry; I would have liked to
erase your memory. It is difficult for me to
construct analogies for that feeling. It was just as
I'm telling you —I would distort the truth by trying
to explain it.

I missed mama so much; the only association I
made was this: mama was dead because of you.
Everyone kept saying that *mama was dead because
of you*. No one ever thought of the effect those
words might have on me.

I had discovered mama's existence after her
death. Everyone has memories of life from a
certain point. For some the first memory is a toy,
for others the smell of a particular food, or a place,
a word, a face, many faces. The first reality that I
have clear knowledge of is mama on her death bed.

Mama had died the night before. There was a
moment on the following afternoon when
grandmother and I were alone in the house with her
body. Grandmother took me by the hand and led
me to her room. There were six candles burning at
the four corners and sides of the bed. The whole
room smelled of burned wax and flowers. Our
shadows grew tall on the walls. On the dresser, in
front of the little statue of Baby Jesus covered by a

glass bell, there were three oil lamps about to go out. The bed was surrounded by wreaths of flowers, except at the head of the bed where grandmother led me. Then I saw mama, *I saw her for the first time.* She had on a black suit, a bouquet of flowers covered half her skirt. She had on a white embroidered blouse, closed at the neck by a blue brooch. In her folded hands was a rosary. The air was heavy — it was a sultry July, the July of 1918, and the room was encased by the shutters, the flowers, the burning candles. The candles were probably placed in a way to light her face. Her face was immobile, severe, slightly sorrowful, like someone who is sleeping and having a disturbing dream. Her black hair, gathered in a ribbon, was pulled back behind her ears. She was white, with a slightly moist pallor. Her head rested on a green cushion, the cushion from the ottoman in the parlor.

As soon as I saw her I was not afraid. "Mama," I said and waited for her to answer me. Grandmother, sobbing behind me, put her hands on my shoulders; one of her tears fell on my neck. I shook my head and it seemed to me that mama also moved. I gripped the head of the bed repeating, "Mama," in a louder voice. Grandmother broke out in a fit of crying; she ran her fingers through my hair, pulling it without realizing it. Suddenly a fly landed on mama's forehead and began working its feet. It took off again, flew back to her face and ended up at the corner of her left eye by her nose. At the head of the bed grandmother waved her hand to chase it away, with no effect. Then making my way between the wreaths on the outside, I reached the bedside and waved my hand in front of mama's face. Because the fly would not budge, I went at it

with my finger. It flew away. *I had touched mama.*
Instinctively I raised her eyelid, seeing her eye —it
was gray with some green flecks. Holding her eyelid in my fingers, I looked at her eye. Grandmother
called me away. Mama's eye remained slightly
open, glassy, empty. Grandmother closed it.

One day, at Villa Rossa, while looking at you I
was happy to discover that your eyes were blue. I
asked tó go to the bathroom off the kitchen. I
looked at myself in the mirror. Each of my eyes
was a different color. The left one was like
mama's.

6

From the day that I saw her on her death bed, with
her head sunk into the green parlor cushion, I
realized mama existed in the world. But alive what
was mama like? What was her voice like? Her
smile? Could mama smile? Did she lean out over
the balcony to hang out the clothes and sing? Did
she put her shopping bag over her arm and go to the
market to bargain with the tradesmen? Did she sit
on the ottoman in the parlor and knit socks, woolen
underpants for winter and mittens with a big thumb,
and then read the newspaper? Did she go out for a
walk on Sunday and have coffee with whipped
cream, go to the movies and enjoy herself? Did
mama also cry? What were her tears like?

They told me, "Your mama was beautiful" and
showed me her photograph. In the photograph
mama was serious, almost frowning. I didn't
recognize her.

In an apartment underneath ours lived a boy named Arrigo. I often went there to play with him; in his house his mother sang, washed the clothes, cooked meals, sprayed perfume on her blouse before going out for a walk; she was in every room, even when she went out, even when in her absence we made more noise or went into the pantry: "If mama finds out!" Arrigo would say. And his mama would find out, yell, give him a slap — but it was different from grandmother's slaps, and it made me mad that Arrigo would cry saying it hurt. I also heard other friends in the apartment house calling, "Mama," from the street or while they ran up the stairs. Their voices were different from mine; it seemed as though their mothers' reply from inside the rooms helped them to go up faster, as if they were flying. They were young women with blond hair or brown who sang; their voices would come from their windows to our balcony. The silence in our house was like that of the villa, but around us were the mothers' voices, the cobbler in his doorway, the sewing machine on the floor above.

"What song did mama sing?" I asked grandmother. "Your mama didn't often sing," she answered. I believed that mama was different from the others.

A little girl, Luisa, came to live on the top floor; her house had a terrace on the roof. Luisa would invite us in. One day she took me aside and said, "When are you going to take me to see your brother?" Arrigo who had overheard us answered for me, "He can't. Some people have taken him. His mama died in childbirth." That made me mad and we had a fist fight. Arrigo made my nose bleed. The next day I had a fever; I had German measles. To make me more comfortable they put me in mama's bed. They said that I spoke of you and of her in my delirium.

7

Your patron's wife would go with us as far as the Gate of San Leonardo where Saint George and the Dragon are carved. Looking up one can see the Fort where the cannon announces noontime. Whom we met on our return depended on the time of year. Astride some wall a farmer would prune the olive trees, taking off his hat to greet the signora; the young share-cropper who had been delivering milk to his city customers would return with his horse-drawn cart; the noise from the horse-collar bells and the jingling of the cans, along with the loudly echoing horse hoofs, would fill the air. The parish priest would close his breviary, using his finger as a bookmark, in order to respond to our homage. We would come upon lovers, not in the least disturbed by our presence; in summer nearly all the girls wore a flower in their hair or carried a bunch of daisies. The street is paved, several meters wide, the walls a little higher than a man, as are the gates to the villas. We would surprise the lovers taking bunches of wisteria, mimosa, oleander hanging over the garden walls. Sometimes boys would take great bunches, to sell in town, I imagine. The signora would threaten them with a stick and ring the gate bells to alert the gardeners, but the boys would have already run off with the flowers, shouting insults at their disturber. Once one of the boys shouted at her, "Old hag!" I laughed and grandmother dealt out a slap. I moved just in time to avoid it, but I realized grandmother did it for appearance's sake as she looked unusually happy. The signora kept repeating, "Bumpkins!"

These were my victories, mine and grandmother's, too, as far as I could tell. She didn't like the signora either. She always said the same thing, repeating how your meeting with the baron had been made possible. "It's all due to me...." she would say, and then add, "If I had only imagined!..." She said that her husband had grown fond of you, and this shouldn't have happened; that you did not deserve it, and after all you weren't their child, and if your father got well and found work he might take you back, what could they expect?

She laughed while she talked, showing her large horse teeth. "It wouldn't be advantageous to take him back, now would it?" Her laugh becoming more cordial, she said, "Don't worry about it, don't worry. For the time being the baby is doing just fine where he is." Her hair was entirely white and she walked slowly, breathing with difficulty. She leaned on a black cane with a silver dog's head on the handle. Grandmother answered humbly, "It's your husband who doesn't want to give him back to us. Is he making the baby suffer? Because we could take him back by force?" "Oh, he wouldn't make him suffer, there's no danger of that...." the signora answered by laughing. She laughed until she had a fit of coughing. One day she said, "It was a lucky thing for the baby that his mother died." Turning red, grandmother said, "Don't say that even if you're joking. Just as we've raised this one," and she held up my hand that she had in hers, "we also know how to raise the next one." She was barely able to add "Good evening," she was so choked up. Going down Costa de' Magnoli she was crying with her lips shut. On Ponte Vecchio I asked her, "Where would he sleep?"

A year had already passed. You wore a petticoat, had curly hair, and your eyes, if possible, were even bluer.

8

Your name, Dante, was given you in honor of your godfather uncle. (On your baptismal day your uncle gave you twelve eggs in a box, each wrapped in a ten lira note.) Your patron did not like the name Dante. Grandmother was unable to get used to your new name; she would call you Dantino. Your patron rebuked her severely: "Now the baby is called Ferruccio. Dante is a common name," he would say to her. Our old grandmother would blush; she would put her finger under your chin, bobbing her head and laughing because you laughed. You repeated her gestures. Without fail the nurse would discover that you had an amazing resemblance to your grandmother.

Now you were a year old. You called your patron papa, his wife mama, the nurse tata. On our visits in the kitchen you would arrive walking in a go-cart or supported by a harness, sometimes held by a maid you seemed very fond of. You always wanted her to carry you, and if she had to leave the kitchen to do her work, you would go after her crying and babbling, "Dida, Dida...." They would put toys in your hand, try everything to distract you except giving you something to eat because it was not time. The nurse, the signora, your patron himself would make desperate faces. Since the baron had guests — afternoon tea — your voice must not be heard; no noise must come from the service rooms. Grandmother was more desperate than anyone; once, compelled to be helpful and to quiet you, she took a pan from the wall and beat on it with a house key. The signora snatched the pan away from her and gave her a shove; grandmother fell into a chair; I shall never forget that incident.

If you cried more than a minute the nurse would carry you away. You would quiet down only if Dida came back. She would come in saying: "Ssss...." also, waving her arms in front of her as though someone were seriously ill just on the other side of the wall. She would be asked if your crying could be heard in the drawing room. At her affirmative reply your patron would leave us. Grandmother apologized as though she were to blame. Dida would calm you down; she had a friendly face, shrewd eyes, country speech, a completely natural character. She was good, like the nurse. It was she who gave me butter and orange marmalade on toast, and often a cup of cold, delicious chocolate. One got the impression that it was hers to dispense; the signora would remain seated at the table, always with her tired manner, as though bored.

9

It was 1920. Day by day they were building around you a prison of affection, habit, complexes inside which —changed by the years and conditions and affections —you would find yourself a prisoner. You escaped from it by your death, even though death is the final liberation or rather the final isolation.

One day during that year 1920, when you were nineteen months old, an attempt was made to change your destiny. Papa had remarried and got a new house, and he decided to take you back with him. After a dramatic interview with your patron, he succeeded in taking you from Villa Rossa and bringing you into his laborer's home. It was a house where the sun shone until three in the afternoon; one of the windows looked onto a garden. Before you arrived they bought a high chair. I lived with our grandparents. I came to visit you, my child's soul full of resentment. Because of you I was forced to be in the presence of our stepmother whom I hated like everything else that *took mama's place.* Our stepmother was young, small, kind, fat and rosy; she did everything she could to get into my good graces.

I came to see you and stayed two days in my father's house. You had a bright color, like an apple; when our stepmother would come in you would clap your hands like I had never seen you do even for Dida. Papa had taught you some words; he had taught you to say beans and butt. You would say: "Deans" and "Dutt." I would ask you, "Do you want to go back to Villa Rossa?" You would say, "No," and shake your head. I would ask you, "Is it better or worse here in papa's house?" You would answer, better. "Etter." All the friends of our stepmother, the neighbors in the apartment, papa's colleagues would fuss over you, and you would smile at everyone and beat your hands on the seat of the high chair. The women would say, "He seems like Baby Jesus. He seems like a big doll. He is the picture of health...." That day you even managed to dissolve my resentment; I took you in my arms and we played together.

I told Luisa I would take her to meet my brother the next day. That morning Luisa showed me the present she had bought for you: a rubber doll that whistled when its belly was squeezed. Because that afternoon she was not sure she could come, she gave me the toy so I could take it to you anyway. But Dida arrived before we did. The door to the stairway was always unlocked. She asked if she could come in and when no one answered she went in. You were alone in the room, in the high chair. Our stepmother was in the kitchen and papa was at work. Dida entered, saw you in the high chair with a little pile of boiled beans in front of you, which you were eating one at a time with satisfaction. A fainting spell came over her; she leaned against the chest of drawers, giving a shout. According to her it was criminal to give you beans to eat, whole ones besides, and unseasoned. She said to our stepmother, now in the room, that she had come to take you back to Villa Rossa. When papa arrived a short time later he found them both crying, each one in a chair.

Papa was at first implacable. He said that the baby was his and that he was grateful to your patron but that this was the way it was: "Is he my son or not?" Dida replied that by reacting that way papa showed he did not love his baby very much, if he would take away his good fortune. She said that the butler was crazy about the boy and that he should give him back now for a while until the patron could be gradually persuaded to give him up. It was a long, pathetic scene, during which, to keep you quiet, our stepmother gave you back your beans. In the face of papa's firmness, Dida emphasized her desperation. She kissed and hugged you, she hid behind the door to try to make you cry as you once did, but to no avail. You ate your beans and waved good-bye. "Now the baby is attached to us," said our stepmother. Dida decided to go away. With a crazed face, bathed in tears, at the point of leaving the house, she said: "I am not going back to the villa without the baby. I would rather jump in the Arno." Her voice was calm at that moment; papa tells: "She gave me the impression she would do what she threatened." Papa went to the window overlooking the street to watch her leave. In the meanwhile he was talking to his wife; both asked themselves if they had the right to decide your life, and in so doing to take away your possibility for an education, for the inheritance the baron would undoubtedly have left you. When Dida appeared in the street, papa called her back. *Your destiny was sealed.*

I arrived with grandmother with Luisa's doll in my hand, but you weren't there. I found the doll eight years later at the bottom of a trunk when grandmother and I had to move. Grandmother gave it to a little boy with red hair who lived on the floor below, in the new house.

19

10

Time makes memories of important events but erases the many actions and words that get us from dawn to sunset. The days of your childhood passed.

It was a childhood lived in a goldfish bowl — without skinned knees, broken toys or dirty faces, with no secrets or discoveries. And with no friends — there in the great silence of the villa. You weren't not allowed to stay in the sun, in too bright a light, nor in a breeze; you weren't allowed to raise your voice, to run about free, nor help yourself to fruit.

The garden was vast, all recesses and corridors of hedges, flower beds, little cypresses and rose bushes; there was a walnut tree on the slope of the Viale, magnolia trees, a pool with red fish and mother-of-pearl; a little Venus enclosed in the green niche held an amphora on her shoulder; a jet of water fell on the shell under the statue. You liked to wander around the greenhouse, looking at the plants in the pots, the artificial vegetation, the big shears and the gardener's tools. The gardener, they said, was your friend; you followed after him while he worked. You brought him the big basket where he put the shrubs, the weeds, the bulbs. You asked the name of each tree and flower and tool, and repeated them out loud so you would remember them. The gardener had a gray mustache, a paternal air, a patient, deliberate manner and way of speaking. You both went around the garden together in the good weather, you asking, he answering and telling you stories from time to time to amuse you. When Dida came looking for you to give you your snack she would find you in the greenhouse; the gardener would be doing his work, you going behind him and listening, handing him the shears, the ruler, the pliers. You were five, six years old, with straight blond hair parted and combed over your forehead. You had nice features, red lips, a pale face, an attentive look fixed in a single expression of amazement and remorse at the same time. You were dressed like a man in short trousers creased in the middle, a jacket buttoned with all three buttons to your neck, a tie. You also talked with a low voice like everyone in the villa. You had acquired the dimension of silence. "A little gentleman," grandmother would tell the neighbors. "He seems like he is English." She would add: "He's growing tall. He's taken after his mother."

Now our visits no longer took place in the kitchen. We went through the door and down the hall into a room with high ceilings, always dimly lit. There was a table in the center of the room, with an ever-flowerless vase on it, which created a zone of light by its reflection. Through the glass doors of the sideboard could be seen the polychrome, decorated service and crystalware. The walls were dark red, amaranth, printed in gold; even the ceiling was decorated. Large, colored, framed prints of a fox hunt hung on the walls: riders with red jackets and white breeches, dogs, foxes fleeing over emerald green meadows, among thickets and very high leafy trees. The writing was in English. In the half-light the prints seemed to be in relief, as though the riders were attached to the wall. In the space between the windows was a photograph of the baron. His face was framed by a beard, cut short and even on his cheeks and under his chin. It was a head and shoulders portrait; his jacket was the same style as yours. We sat near the window, making a kind of semi-circle in the chairs.

The years went by without changing anything, except that you and I grew up. The others stayed the same: grandmother in her humbled position, your patron with his paternal and severe tone, the veiled sarcasm of the signora. Dida had grown fatter and knew how to laugh without breaking the silence. She would fix a snack for both of us. Even the sandwiches were the same — bread, butter and orange marmalade. Then you and I would go out into the garden.

11

One day, forced by need, papa came to your patron to ask for three hundred lire. Three hundred lire was a lot in those days. He wanted the money to buy a used tail-coat from an old clothes dealer, as he had found work at the "Gambrinus," where the waiters wore tuxedos. Papa worked as a waiter in cafes. With the little money remaining, the family gave themselves a day in the country. There were thirty coins. From that day on papa never set foot again in Villa Rossa. Now your patron was sure of having definitely conquered you; to his wife's amusement, he had added another argument. Grandmother bit her lip every time the episode was brought up. She promised herself that she would pay father's debt with her savings: she earned one lira an hour for her half-day's work. I played a coin-tossing game on the street with my friends; three hundred lire was a sum to make us laugh, it seemed so enormous. Grandmother and I would have supper together, coffee and milk, and spend one lire each.

It was after the incident of the loan that your patron wouldn't allow mama to be mentioned in your presence.

And so you and I would go into the garden. You would walk along beside me, always a bit detached. You treated me with the ostentatious condescension of a child; you always frowned, as though you considered me an enemy. You had me observe the trees, the flowers, the fish in the pool with the haughtiness of a boy who lets another of the same age admire his toys in order to impress him and make him envious, but never lets him touch them. You led me often and happily to the greenhouse to see the turtles. On the day when I turned one over on its back with my foot you began to cry. Not even the gardener could quiet you; you insulted me between sobs. You called the turtle Beatrice.

You almost ran back to the house; your patron slapped me, grandmother took my side. "Wretch," the signora exclaimed. "He'll have a fever to-night," your patron said; he looked at me with hateful eyes. I was no longer afraid of him. The visits to Villa Rossa seemed like a play. I lived a different life, spending many hours a day on the street. To come to Villa Rossa was an adventure for me, a double existence that I kept secret from my friends.

I was ten years old and grandmother didn't hold me by my hand any longer. When we left the villa I

veered off the path to Via San Leonardo. I would
go into the farmers' courtyard, I would yell, I
would ring the bells of the villas, I would gather
the olives fallen from the trees. On the times when
the signora walked with us I would misbehave on
purpose and she would threaten me with her cane.
While saying good-bye grandmother would beg the
signora not to tell her husband about my behavior.
She was a strange woman, the signora; she would
often give me a caress, like a reproach.

12

The gardener promised to give me a piece of cane.
I said that grandmother needed it to hang out the
laundry. It was really for me and my friends to
make pea shooters for launching paper cones: at the
tip of the cone we put a pin with the point sticking
out. We blew into the tube and aimed at girls'
behinds.

The first time you asked me about mama was the
day the gardener gave me the cane.

It was a nice cane, solid, yellow, with green
stripes, empty inside like I wanted. From the
gardener's smile when he gave me the cane I knew
that he and I understood each other; if not about the
pins, then certainly about the pea shooter.

You were then six years old. So I was eleven. It
was early in autumn, that is to say the autumn of
1924. The gardener left us; he was wearing a straw
hat with a dirty gray ribbon, a dark blue apron tied
behind his neck and back. He went out of the
greenhouse with the rubber hose to do some

watering. We were sitting in the empty greenhouse window. You were wearing a dotted blue tie. You took the cane from my hand, saying "I gave you this cane." My first impulse was to grab the cane away, but I restrained myself so as not to compromise my conquest. "All right," I imagine I said to you. "Do you want to give it back?" Even sitting down you were shorter than I; you were pale and seemed blonder than ever, golden blond, beautiful, you were like light itself; because of this the resentful look you gave me acquired a particular maliciousness.

"I'll give it back on one condition," you told me, adding, "Who was mama?"

You puffed out your cheeks and I didn't know if you were really laughing or being serious. I saw the cane in your hands, it was as though I had forgotten it. In front of us was a hedge that circled a little lawn: between us and the hedge, the sidewalk of the greenhouse, then a section of gravel. Below the hedge a lizard stuck his head out. It hesitated a moment and then crossed the gravel. I took advantage of it to change the subject: "Look, look at the lizard," I said, "let's get it!" I made like I was going after it, but you remained seated. You balanced the cane on your thighs. You repeated, "Are you going to tell me who mama was?"

"If I tell you you'll go repeat it and then cry," I replied.

"Tell me who she was," you insisted.

I said, "She was the mama of both of us."

"Is she dead?"

"Yes, she's dead."

"Was her name Nella?"

"How did you know?"

Then you got up laughing; you had two front teeth much larger than the others — perhaps the others had fallen out. You still had your baby teeth. You handed me the cane and stood up, walking toward the gardener who was watering the lawn. You said to him, "You're right, her name was Nella."

He nodded his head and smiled. You had your usual look, remorseful and amazed at the same time, a cautious attitude.

The second time you brought up that subject was in an automobile, during the following winter.

At a certain time in the afternoon a son of your patron, on his free time, would come to take you for a drive in the car. If it happened during one of our visits, you would say good-bye. That day your patron was in town with the baron, in another automobile driven by the second son. Dida suggested that I go along. You were unusually happy to have me with you. The chauffeur was thirty years old, with a prominent chin and black eyes; he was distinctive, with a distinction belonging to a servant, to the master's chauffeur. Even he, in his element of silence, laughed without a sound coming from his mouth. He had a cap with a visor and a cape with an astrakhan collar. You usually sat in the front with him; that day we sat in the back. We watched him drive from behind the glass. You were wearing a tobacco-colored overcoat, a gray wool scarf around your neck, a hat like a man's on your head. It was the first time I had been in an automobile.

We went down the viales. The sun was pale, the trees bare, heaps of dead leaves were on the

sidewalks.   I looked out the window and the
unusual perspective made familiar places seem
unfamiliar: the Chalet Fontana, the Giramontino,
the Porte Sante. The car went at a moderate speed;
every once in a while the driver would turn and
smile at us; his incisors were a little protruding.
We sat quietly next to one other.

Suddenly,   before   we   reached   Piazzale
Michelangelo, you said, as though to yourself, but
with the intention of being overheard: "She died
when I was very young."

"Yes, you were barely a month old," I replied.

"Is it true that she died crazy?"

"What do you mean, crazy?"

"She died crazy, didn't she?"

"No, that's not true. She died from the flu."

"She didn't either.   She was crazy, I know.
You're a liar."

"Who told you that?"

"My Papa told me."

"He told you a lie."

"You're a liar. Shut up. I don't want to see you
any more."

You screamed; you knocked on the glass for the
car to stop. You had become red in the face and
looked at me with eyes full of hate. "What did you
do?" your chauffeur-brother asked me. He stopped
the car.

"Nothing," I answered.

You said, "I want to go back home." You went
to sit next to him.

13

Everything that happened on our visits to Villa Rossa was unconnected with my life. It existed in a dimension of things and in a world that didn't belong to me, a game and a play, as I said. While I was there I too entered into the play. I played my part intensely, but as soon as I went away, as soon as I entered into my own reality, everything faded away until it disappeared. You were already a memory; and your patron, his wife, Dida, were erased from my mind almost immediately. One day, on Via San Leonardo, I saw a young farmer follow his love rival, brandishing a pitchfork. The gardener ran to disarm the would-be assassin. Taken from the surroundings of the villa, the gardener was a different man, a man like others; one who raised his voice and made excited gestures. He was outside the play. I seemed to see him for the first time.

Even our talks about mama didn't leave a deep impression on me. Affection for our mama had found its place in my spirit; it had become a selfish affection, shut off from and indifferent to any external violence. I had already begun to invent mama for myself. I dreamed about her and gave her a face different from the one she had on her deathbed. I invented her smile, I imagined her crying. In my dream her clothes were the same: the black suit, the lace blouse, the blue brooch. Sometimes I would meet women in the street who could have been her. I would overtake them so I could look at them again, my heart beating furiously, but always in each one of them there was something that made me change my mind. Now I know it was something in their eyes, in their look. They were *alive*. I couldn't disassociate mama from death.

Not even the upsetting words you spoke in the automobile and during the first moments while we were going back to the villa made a deep impression on me. Even they stayed in the limbo of the play, in the game of roles controlled by the personality of your patron. "It's your fault mama died:" this thought was now clear and constant in me, but I didn't hate you anymore because of it. I was used to the idea that mama had to die. That you were the cause of it seemed like fate to me. It was part of the mystery that circumfused the person of mama that I had seen for the first time on her deathbed. You, in that sense, belonged to her. *You were dead with her.*

Part Two

14

For the next eight years we rarely saw each other. I was working as an errand boy and didn't have Thursdays free any more. Then you left Villa Rossa. The baron died, and because his heirs who had come to live in the Villa intended to limit the responsibilities of your patron, he quit. (Dida must not have pleased them either. She disappeared from the house and from your life.) Immediately after quitting he took you for a long vacation on the Riviera. San Remo, Montecarlo. It lasted for more than two years. Perhaps he hoped to find in his old age — still vigorous and slightly tempted by the innocent notion of freedom — a taste of youth that he had never had. Or perhaps he was merely trying to heal a painful wound before putting himself at the service of a new master in another Villa Rossa.

You were the only person capable of consoling his solitude; the only one, since the baron's death, on whom he could exercise his own dictatorship, the only one he could *serve and love.* He surrounded you with an excessive, almost aggressive affection; he washed you, dressed you, put on your boots, cleaned your nails, combed your hair — as though you were a toddler instead of a boy of ten. He taught you to eat certain things at certain times, to amuse yourself at a precise time and place, to bow and to give an order, to enjoy every comfort and at the same time to harbor an infinite number of inhibitions. The conditions you experienced in infancy were perpetuated in adolescence. *You never discovered anything with your own eyes.* And so you lived constantly alone, but not alone with yourself, *alone with him;* your thoughts were those he suggested to you. In exchange you gave him an affection mixed with veneration and fear, you modeled yourself after him as he desired, and you made his virtue of order yours, his imperious defects yours; he called these your caprices.

We came to visit you, grandmother and I, in the place that your patron —once the vacation was over —had rented outside Porta Romana. (In this house his wife died.) It was a basement apartment, and there was a little orchard between it and the street, a few square meters suitable for a garden: cages of canaries, a stunted rose bush, two old turtles. You had become aware of the difference of our situations. The impatience that my presence and grandmother's aroused in you was obvious by your attitude. It was even reflected physically, in your gestures, in your tone of voice, your condescension, that correct and particular cordiality with which your patron had always treated us.

In all those years we never spoke of mama; you and I never spoke alone. You grew, but you were always the same. Every time I brought back this impression: you were growing taller, your body was developing harmoniously, but you were always the same. You always resembled yourself, you were a copy of Ferruccio in the garden at Villa Rossa, like a photograph continually being enlarged. Even your clothes always seemed the same, of an impeccable style. The same with your eyes and blond hair. The day I read that the clothes of Jesus grew as he grew, I thought of you. And you grew up thin, pale, in delicate health, suffering often from tonsillitis. I was now eighteen years old, didn't know what I believed, and went to live alone in a rented room. I began to study; I didn't go to see you anymore, but limited my visiting to grandmother who was in a home for the aged poor. She would save her snack for me.

You and I lived in the same town, but it was as though we were separated by an ocean. I no longer believed that it was your fault mama died. *I had forgotten you.*

15

It was 1935. At that time you were not quite seventeen, because it was January or February; I was twenty-two. The damp cold was intense. Usually, when the library closed, I would go back to my room; I would go out late at night to find my vagabond friends. But on certain evenings when I couldn't stand the cold, I would go to the billiard cellars where the rooms were heated.

It had rained and my feet were soaked; the heat of the place made me shiver. The billiard rooms were crowded, perhaps it was a Saturday evening, and there wasn't even room enough to lean against the walls. I heard noises coming from the ping-pong room where the young high-school boys met and where I never went. We called it "the

kindergarten." I pushed open the door to see if
there was room to sit down. The room was small,
and about twenty young boys crowded around the
table, leaving the necessary space for the players.
Near the door was an empty chair, next to the
radiator. I closed the door behind me and sat
down. Some of the young spectators turned around,
surprised that I came in there. To them I was an
outsider, one of the billiard players, and poorly
dressed besides, with rather uncared-for hair and
beard, a thin, shabby overcoat, a wild look. They
were junior-high and high-school students, noisy,
happy with the first freedom they had been able to
grab.

I was huddled up trying to stop shivering, hands
in my coat pockets, chin on my chest. The players
were warming up with a volleying that rose above
the spectators' din. The little ball made a tick-tock
that thundered in my head louder than screams. A
boy wearing the Fascist Youth uniform, black shirt
with white braids, came to get the fez he had left
on the radiator. It was a childish gesture of
distrust; I raised my head to look at the ill-
mannered boy and absentmindedly glanced around
the room. It was then I saw you. You were one of
the two players standing right in front of me. Your
height made you tower over the others. Seated as I
was, I could see only your face and half your body.
You were hot, a curly lock caressing your forehead;
between each stroke you would straighten up
quickly. I hadn't seen you for several years and was
surprised by how much you had grown. You had
really grown, that is, you had changed a little. You
were more robust, your shoulders and chest had
become wider, your figure was more decisive; you

looked like a premature adult. Your hair had even grown darker.

You had a hard, almost cruel expression, such was the attention you gave the game; your eyes followed the trajectory of the little ball with an intensity that was almost ferocious; you hit the ball moving your forearm, turning your shoulder only on the return shot. One could see that you were a good, well-trained player, and that your prestige was involved in the match. I realized it better when I discovered that the audience was against you; at every shot you missed there rose a great clamor of satisfaction and encouragement for your adversary. I believe his name was Mario.

When a point was contested you had everyone against you. You would try to justify it, looking around and saying, "That was inside, the point is mine." You would look around for support that no one gave you. But your voice was uncertain, your gaze distracted. You would say, "All right," with a condescension that had the taste of tears; you would ask the adversary to continue the game. Only when the ball was in motion did you find your fierce calm, your obstinacy. You won the match. After making the point that gave you the victory, you triumphantly tossed the paddle on the table with a gesture that seemed angry. Your only words were "Pay up."

I got up, standing behind your adversary. He threw two lire over the net. The others who had bet also paid you. The member of the Fascist Youth said: "I'll pay you tomorrow." "Give it to me now, because I know you have it," you replied. You moved toward him, sure of purpose, when your eyes met mine. You flushed to your hair, smiled, and then immediately turned away. I understood that you were not pleased to see me.

In answer to you the Fascist Youth made a challenge. "If you'll give me eight to twenty," he said, "we can play ten lire." To protect yourself you refused the advantage, but the spectators fell upon you as one. You didn't know how to react. You took up the paddle and made the first shot. You kept looking my way; you were so excited and distracted that you missed the first three shots and lost the first point.

I was now in the front row, and saw that everyone was somewhat irritated by my presence. They weren't sure why I was in their midst, in the kindergarten. A short boy with glasses provoked hilarity by saying, "We have visitors." At that moment you missed a beginning stroke and lost the first match. Halfway through the second one you put down the paddle and declared yourself beaten: "I'm late," you said. Unexpectedly everyone protested, begging you to go on. You put on your overcoat and they took it off you. "It's impossible for you to lose to such a bozo," somebody said. Even the Fascist said: "I haven't even won yet!" surprised by his own good fortune.

Then you said very brusquely, "My brother is waiting for me."

A burst of laughter. "Since when did you have a brother?" they asked you. "You're a fool, that's what you are. You've got no character!" "You're stuck up," others said.

You could only repeat, "My brother!"

"He has to run to see his girlfriend," someone said.

"Signorina Franchi!" another said.

And everyone began to chant: "Fran-chi Fer-ruc-cio!"

Now you had your hat on, and your face was twisted. You shouted: "There's my brother, that one!" pointing a finger at me. Silence suddenly descended. Everyone stood still and you took that opportunity to leave. Mario, the boy who had played against you earlier, asked me, "Are you really his brother?"

"Me? No way!" I answered.

"Ferruccio is an idiot," he said.

"Id-i-ot!" the others repeated.

Leaving the room I saw that you were going up the stairs slowly, expecting me to follow you. Instead I went toward the opposite room and hid behind the door that had a window looking into the card room. You had turned back and were looking for me among the people milling around and the billiard players; after a second search you went away. You were wearing a brown overcoat, a gray scarf, a Tyrolean-type hat.

16

The room I had sublet was nine feet long and five feet wide — like a cell, in fact. The window was not a window, but an outward sloping hole. I had furnished it with a small bed, a table and a chair. Cleaning was not included in the rent, and I wasn't very neat then. I had only one sheet large enough to use as a top and bottom sheet, so when I decided to get it washed I was left without one. And I had only one blanket. Because my overcoat didn't provide much additional warmth, I always slept in my clothes, wrapping my feet in an undershirt.

The room gathered a lot of dust, which I removed only from the table, and not even from that very often. In the summer the air was unbreathable; it got the sun all day. I would go completely nude, my rear sticking to the chair. But winter was worse —I couldn't protect myself from the cold. Once in a while, on her free afternoon, grandmother would come to tidy up, but I didn't want her to because it was trouble for her, and she did nothing but complain and scold me. Finally I told her I had gone back to work and had rented a nice furnished apartment with heat and a cleaning lady. I invented some address and told her not to come see me because I was never at home. She thought I was ashamed of her uniform. But she couldn't resist the temptation. One day, at the old folks home, she told me she had gone to that address but no one knew me.

"You got the address wrong," I told her. But I couldn't keep it up, so I told her I had found work in Rome. This time I gave her the address of a friend of mine there and sent him letters to mail; he would return those that grandmother sent to me. I hadn't seen her since Christmas; that winter, the second one I spent in those conditions, was hard on me. I didn't want to give her other worries by seeing what a bad state I was in.

It was an afternoon in March, toward seven in the evening. For two days we were without electricity because the landlady hadn't paid the bill. I was reading by candlelight when I heard a knock at the door; I blew out the candle and didn't answer since I thought it was the landlady coming for the back rent. I heard her calling, I heard her try the handle. Then she went away. I went to the door to eavesdrop and heard her saying, "If you want to leave a message!" And your voice: "Tell him his brother came."

Then, on an impulse I turned the key and the handle at the same time. Fear had turned to joy. I called, "Ferruccio!"

The landlady, a good soul, paused at the door with a lighted candle in her hand. She said to you: "You're his brother? He told me only of his grandmother." It seemed to me you were blushing. I tried to get you out of your predicament by saying to her, "All right, signora, thank you. Good evening." But she kept on stalling and added, "See how your brother lives? Try to get him to be less of a bear. What would it cost me to straighten up his room a little? But he doesn't want anyone to go in, and when he goes out he takes the key with him!"

I was on tenterhooks; you, head bowed, hat in your hand, were embarrassed. "All right, signora, good evening," I repeated. She went away and I sighed. You were still standing in the middle of the room with your hat in your hand. The first thing you said was, "She's a nice person. Why do you treat her like that?"

We were left in the dark. I said, "We'll have to call her back to light the candle."

"I have a match," you replied.

17

The candle was stuck in the neck of an old bottle of Kummel; it was near the end, but the wick burned brightly enough. You took the only chair and I sat by leaning against the edge of the table.

"Well," I said, smiling, with affectionate irony. "To what do I owe this honor?"

You put the leather bag that you had in your hand on the bed behind you, resting your hat on your knee. I asked you in the same tone: "What can I do for you?"

"You can let me stay here for a little while. Tomorrow I'll bring a bed, if you don't mind."

"Of course!" I replied.

I was surprised, but above all your natural manner impressed me, and especially the familiar way you treated me — like a friend, I thought. In those first five minutes we covered the distance that for sixteen years had separated us.

"*My father* has become very stubborn," you said.

"What do you mean? If you don't explain yourself I can't let you stay. I'll have to take you back home."

"We aren't staying anymore in the place you knew. Now we live on Borgognissanti, in an sublet room."

You were dressed as you were two months ago, but without your scarf. I had avoided that place since that time. The winter hadn't hurt you; you were solid and filled out, you seemed sure of yourself. The candlelight shone on your face and I could see your calm expression. You had some down on your cheeks and over your lip: it's blondness stood out in relief in that light.

I couldn't picture you and *him* in a sublet room. "Let's get back to the point," I said.

"What?"

"It's an expression. If I said *ab ovo* would you understand me better?"

"Do you know Latin?"

"No, unfortunately.... Don't you think you'll change your mind? Do you want me to go back with you?"

"I won't go back tonight for sure."

"What happened?"

"It's all because of a girl."

"Oh!" was all I could think of saying. Then I added, "You've changed a lot."

The candle gave a last sputter; I made it last longer by collecting the wax that was stuck on the bottle. You said, "She's the daughter of the landlady. There's nothing between us. We just kid around. This morning *my father* caught us in the hall. He shut me up in our room and chased her with a broom." You smiled. "There was a big argument with her parents. In the meantime I found a way to get out."

A little later the candle went out permanently. You lit a little wax match and I said, "Let's go out and buy another candle. We have to eat anyway."

"If you don't mind, I'd like to treat you," you said.

18

I lived on Via Ricasoli, next to the safety exit of the movie house "Modernissimo." It was late in the evening, perhaps nine o'clock. Across the street, the globe of a dairy bar was lighted; from the illuminated second floor came dance music. It was still cold and the moon and stars were out. At the end of the street, directly in front of us, the dome and the apse of Santa Maria del Fiore were framed. We passed the building of the local newspaper, *La Nazione,* and turned into the Piazza del Duomo.

"How did you get my address?" I asked.

"I asked at the Registry Office!" You were smiling.

"Do you feel like a real supper?"

"In the evening I usually eat lightly. We could eat something standing up at 'Becattelli'."

You were really different from what I had always thought; you were a friend. I took you by the arm.

The place was almost deserted. Giovanni Becattelli sat at the cashier's desk with his listless air. Two customers stood eating from their plates on the marble counter. Sitting at the only table was the newspaper vendor of Piazza Vittorio and his wife, both fat and perhaps suffering from dropsy, and the old tie salesman who had pains in his arms and legs.

"Do you come here often?" I asked you.

"The owner's son was my friend from school."

Giovanni brightened upon seeing us enter; at first he didn't know we were together.

"Ciao," he said to you. "How come you're still out at this hour?"

You were a little embarrassed, but you recovered your natural reserve. "I'm with my brother," you said.

Giovanni shook his head, and he too, like your friends, said, "Since when is he your brother?"

"Since we were born," I said.

We had to show him our identification cards to convince him. We ate a bowl of pasta and a sandwich. You drank a sweet white wine.

No grocery stores were open so we had to walk around for quite a while to find a candle. We ended up in Via de' Neri. A number 13 red streetcar was standing in front of us. I said to you, "Why don't you get on this streetcar and go back home. Get off at the Ponte alla Carraia. *Your father* will be worried.

"I left him a note."

"It's my duty to take you back. Everything will be all right by now."

The grocer lowered his steel shutters with a bang; an icy wind swept down Via della Ninna that made us shudder. You were silent and pale. Suddenly you said, "Good evening!" and turned your back, running away quickly. Crossing Via Altafronte along the Arno you were already ahead of me by fifty meters. A tram cut in front of you at Ponte alle Grazie, so I was able to catch up with you.

We turned toward each other. A very strong wind struck us at the intersection. You coughed. "You're heated up and will catch cold. Is your throat always bad?" I asked you.

Your silence continued. You looked at me stealthily. I saw flashes of resentment in your eyes. I offered to buy you a coffee in a bar at Canto alle Rondini. You accepted, still enclosed in your obstinate silence and resentment. You straightened your tie in front of a mirror advertisement. Then you ran a stream of water over the spoon before stirring the sugar in your cup. The bartender, a friend of mine, said: "Our dear friend is a hygienist!" Blushing, you gave him a crushing look.

On Via della Pergola, in front of the theater, was a long row of carriages. A noisy group of young men came out of a house of prostitution. "All right, you can stay with me," I said. "Are you happy? But tomorrow morning early we're going to Borgognissanti."

Silence. "Do you understand?"

You replied, "Uh huh!"

19

We had bought two candles and I lit them both. You sat on the edge of the bed.

"I'm getting you into a mess," you said. You were sure of yourself again and seemed happy. The expression on your face had softened and become almost childlike; you talked like a victorious little child.

"You know what *your father* thinks of me," I said. "He will say that I talked you into not going back."

"I left him a note that I would come back only after I found a new room."

Our shadows filled the room; the room had a rather high ceiling making it seem more empty and shabby. Under the window was a chest with family things grandmother had passed on to me. On the table some books, among them a large nineteenth-century volume of the complete works of Du Musset, in the original.

You picked up the Musset, resting it on your knees to open it.

"Do you know French?"

"I'm trying to learn by reading it," I answered.

"Without a grammar?"

"I have a little dictionary." I picked it up from the opposite end of the table and showed it to you.

"I use Fiorentino's grammar; I could lend it to you."

"How advanced are you?"

"I was failed because of French last year."

"You failed the year just for one subject?"

You still had your childish tone; it seemed like you were resting, or that you had discarded an attitude.

"And mathematics."

"Ah!"

"And my Italian orals didn't go well. I took a seven for the written part."

"What did *your father* say? He must have blamed it on ping-pong!"

"More or less."

"And on the girl! What's her name?"

You blushed and I understood that you would rather not answer, but did so out of a sense of gratitude.

"Giuliana."

"And what's she like?" It was just as though I were talking with a friend. "How old is she?"

"Eighteen."

"She's older than you, then. A real woman."

I understood that it had gone too far, and that it was difficult to earn your confidence. I was thinking that *you were my brother for the first time*. You reached out for the picture on the table that was propped against the bottle under the candle.

"That's mama," I said.

You took the photograph, holding it so the light would fall on it. I watched your face, but saw nothing. It seemed like you were paying attention to the photograph to please me.

You said: "The one grandmother has is clearer."

There was a pause; we were stumped for something to say for different reasons. You got up and I put the photograph back in place.

"I don't have an extra sheet," I said. "Do you want to go to bed?"

"If you don't mind."

You took off your overcoat and hung it on the handle of the window by the loop at the neck. You opened your leather bag where you had packed pajamas, bedroom slippers wrapped in a newspaper, a towel, toothpaste, all the essentials.

"Where will you sleep?" you asked.

"I'll fix something on the chair."

"All night? We could sleep together, both on our sides, if you don't mind."

"Maybe later. I want to study as long as the candle lasts, if you don't mind." I laughed. "You're teaching me," I told you. You still didn't understand. "Didn't you notice that without meaning to I also said, 'if you don't mind'?"

There was only one chair in the room. "Take it," I said. "I'll sit on the chest. It's high enough if I sit up straight."

You put your jacket on the back of the chair, arranging the shoulders; you folded your pants at the pleat with a practiced gesture. When you were in your underpants I saw your long legs, a little thin at the knees, very white. Then you came toward the table in your pajamas, with the towel folded over your arm. "Where's the bathroom?" you asked.

"There is no real bathroom. We wash in the kitchen; you have to cross the house and the others are sleeping. However...."

"All right," you said, annoyed.

20

I put out one of the two candles to give you less bother and also so I could have light as long as possible. A little later I could tell you were asleep by the way you were breathing. I lit a cigarette and began studying. From time to time some carriages or automobiles would pass on the street. In the intervals of silence I heard the muffled music from the movie house. Then a steel shutter was lowered: the bar on the corner of Via de' Pucci was closing, then the movie house let out, after that the solitary footsteps of the night watchman. It was the time when I usually joined my friends. I was afraid that if you woke up and didn't see me you would go through the streets looking for me. I decided to go out just long enough to leave a note at the cafe five minutes away. I wrote a few lines. Carefully I began to get up, holding the chest with one hand in fear that it would move.

You said: "Why did you put grandmother in the old folks home?"

Your words were so unexpected that they seemed to be spoken by another person. I sat down again on the chest and fiddled with the note I had written.

You added, "It's a shame." Your voice was a little hoarse because you had just woken up, but I could tell you had been thinking about it and weren't talking in your sleep.

"Why do you think it's a shame?" I asked you.

"People will speak badly of you."

"What do you mean?"

You had said "people" as though you had said *my father*.

"Look, Ferruccio, people are happy to judge without becoming involved in the situation."

"I don't understand."

"Then listen: who do you think loves grand-mother more — me or other people."

"I think you do."

"Then you also think that I would take better care of grandmother than other people would, isn't that right?"

"I'm sleepy and you're hard to follow."

"Listen. Grandmother couldn't work any longer. You know she's more than seventy. I was earning fifteen lire a day. It's a salary, but we just couldn't get along on it. Grandmother would get tired just trying to cook something. One time she got sick and I had to take her to the hospital and she only had a little bronchitis. I had to be at work all day long, and I couldn't be with her or afford a nurse....

At the home they take care of her and...do you understand me?"

"Can I ask a question?"

"Go ahead."

"It isn't because you didn't want to work, is it?"

"In a way, yes. I want to do a different work."

"Is it true you want to be a writer?"

"I want to be a journalist."

"And can you do it?"

"I hope so."

Now you were talking half in your sleep. "But if you've never even been to school!"

"So what?"

"If you don't even have the Fiorentino grammar!"

"Aren't you going to lend me yours?"

"My father says you're a good-for-nothing — he says we're the same breed, you and I."

"That's right, we are the same breed. What do you think of that?"

"That *my father* is right."

I lit a cigarette. I had already smoked three and the room was full of smoke.

"Does the smoke bother you? I'm thinking about your sore throat."

"I don't have a sore throat."

"Years ago you spent a lot of time in bed with tonsillitis."

"After that I had an operation...."

Silence. Then unexpectedly, just like a few minutes earlier, you said, "So why does grandmother do nothing but cry when we go to see her?"

"You've been to see grandmother?"

"Today, too, to ask for your address. She told me you were in Rome, but I saw you the other day on Via Strozzi. I understood then that you had abandoned her."

You had turned on your side and were looking at me with your head raised.

"I don't want you to think so badly of me," I told you.

"Why don't you go back to work? Why don't you become a billiard marker, for example?"

"That's an idea.... How long have you been going to see grandmother?"

"For a couple of months, from that day we saw each other at the ping-pong game. I was sorry for behaving that way, and after I realized you ran away from me, I wanted to do better by going to see grandmother...."

I got up and gave you a kiss.

21

The candle had nearly burned to the end. I lit another and you said, "Why don't you come to bed?"

I took off my overcoat and scarf and blew out the candle.

"Aren't you going to get undressed?"

"I'll sleep in my clothes, if you don't mind."

"You said 'if you don't mind,' eh?"

We both lay on our sides, face to face; our legs touched; you had to keep your knees bent because the bed wasn't long enough for you. And once again, following a thought, after a silence I had kept thinking you had gone to sleep, you said: "You take after *our mother*, but more like the photograph that grandmother has than the one on your table. I don't. I take after *our father*." (From that time on we always said our mother, our father.)

"What memories do you have of our mother?" I asked you.

"None. Grandmother has spoken to me about her."

"I talked to you about her, at Villa Rossa, when we were children. Don't you remember?"

"Vaguely."

"That day when the gardener gave me the cane...."

"Nando?"

"Yes, Nando.... And a second time in the automobile, and you said...."

"What did I say?"

"That you didn't love her."

"If you say so.... What was she like?"

"She was beautiful, you know!"

"You say she was beautiful to mean you are beautiful, too!"

"Her eyes seemed green and she always looked serious. Like you do when you play ping-pong."

"What am I like when I play?"

"You seem far away from everyone, with only one thing on your mind, as though out of this world and against the world."

"I don't understand.... Were her eyes green or did they just seem green. Don't your remember her very well?"

"Well, in the sense of having known her well, no. But I remember her face very well."

"What did she do?"

"What do you mean, do?"

"Each day."

"She lived, and then she died."

"See, you don't remember! Even grandmother can't tell me anything exact. How can I become fond of her if you both can't tell me anything about her?"

"But she was *our mother!*"

"Yes, and then?"

"She died when you were twenty-five days old."

"I know. And Clorinda, the one with the milk, took me to Villa Rossa...."

"That's right, her name was Clorinda!"

"She's still alive but doesn't live on San Leonardo any longer. A lot of things have changed in that neighborhood.... So her eyes were green. Grandmother told me she was tall, and that I resemble her in this. *Our father* is a little shorter than average. See, I am like her, too."

"She liked oranges."

"And orange marmalade, too?"

"I think so."

"How do you know that?"

"I've asked grandmother, too. But she can't tell much more.... And she couldn't stand stale bread. Grandmother said that it was awful during the war."

"And?"

"She loved dark clothes."

"And?"

"She liked comedies about Stenterella."

"And?"

"She couldn't stand big crowds. So she never went to see the fireworks outside the Duomo at Easter."

"Did grandmother tell you that?"

"Yes."

"And?"

"And...she was a good seamstress, did you know that?"

"Uhm, uhm!"

"She worked for a tailor on a little square halfway down Via del Corso."

"Where the Hotel Sasso di Dante is?"

We talked, lying quietly in order to conserve the heat our bodies produced. It was late. The light of the moon came through the window weakly, like a tenuous dawn. At times your breath touched my face, which pleased me, and I tried to get closer to it. We heard horns blowing intermittently for a few minutes at a time. "Those are the delivery trucks of *La Nazione* running to early trains with newspapers still wet with fresh ink," I said. I was happy with you beside me; happy to get to know you, happy because you were next to me and you were my friend and we were talking. We were talking about mama and about many other things.

Then you fell asleep, breathing a little harshly. Voices on the street drew closer and I could tell they were my friends. When they reached my building they began calling me insistently, waking the whole block, so that I decided to get up. I took the note from the table that I had wanted to take to the cafe; opening the window, I motioned for them to be quiet, and threw down the note.

One of them read it aloud; a collective laugh and vulgar exclamations were bellowed in my direction. One of them said: "Kiss *her* behind her ear for me, your brother!"

You continued sleeping, as tranquil as though in your own bed. When I came back you turned over on your other side, saying something in your sleep that I didn't understand.

22

A noise coming from the window woke us at the same time. Outside a man in a sling tied to a rope had rested his foot on the windowsill, striking the windowpane. He was fixing the pipe that channels rain water from the roof. Such a way of waking up put us immediately in good humor.

You had gone to bed wearing your wristwatch. "*My father* would make trouble over something like that," you said. Then you added: "Let's get up and go to Canossa to face the music," and you started laughing.

"You know your history," I said.

The landlady and the other tenants had gone out; I took you to the kitchen so you could wash. Then, after you had put all your things back in your bag, we went out.

"Shall we have breakfast?" you asked. "You must let me pay."

"You're really rich," I said.

"Ping-pong pays well." You blushed this time, too; it was clear that you were changing, that you were in a state of passage, and every time that the essential you in formation discovered itself in its actions and in its reckless postures, the essential you called itself back to order.

We went into a dairy bar behind the prefecture: coffee with milk and toasted bread.

"Butter?" asked the owner who served us at a table.

"Yes."

She returned with two portions of butter and marmalade and more bread.

"I brought some more marmalade to save myself another trip," she said.

She was a young, open woman, with an exciting look and manner. I knew her and liked her, and she knew it and joked with me.

You asked her, "Don't you have any orange marmalade?"

"Only in the jar. If you're dying for it I can open one."

"Good. Make him happy," I said. "Did you know he's my brother?"

"I would have sworn it," she said.

"We're nothing alike," you exclaimed so suddenly as to seem discourteous.

"So you say," she replied. "You both look like you know what's what!" She went toward the counter and I watched your eyes follow her: you looked at her like a teenager who knows what a woman is, with a teenager's desire. I wanted to say something, but the words died on my lips. Now I was intimidated, and I think it was my time to blush.

She came to our table with the jar; she turned to you and said: "Your brother is a poet, but he wakes up in the morning like a laborer."

Someone at a table nearby tapped on his glass with a spoon. She left us, after dishing the marmalade onto little plates. As she walked away she threw me a look and smiled. I said to her, "Always hot, eh?"

"At the boiling point," she replied, and smiled more openly. It was our way of joking.

And when we called her again, to pay the bill, she said to you, "Don't pay any attention. Your brother and I are good friends."

"Do you know her well?" you asked me after we had walked a while in silence. "Did you take me there because she's your lover?"

You were red again, but your blue eyes were smiling; you were giving me the gift of complicity — unnecessary, but it established a definite friendship between us. I was sorry to have to disappoint you; you didn't believe me.

We were on Via Parione, and before reaching Borgognissanti you stopped abruptly: it was as if the street that opened before us with its hotels on one side and its row of narrow shops on the other had suddenly recalled you to reality. It was as though, for a few seconds, you were making a different face for yourself from what you had, a different expression. You returned to your previous self, and I thought you were a hypocrite, but immediately after I thought that you were unhappy. You said: "It's better for me to go alone; believe me."

"I'll stay outside the door for a while, in case you need me."

You smiled faintly.

"Will you come see me again?" I asked you.

"Let's meet at grandmother's on Thursday."

You were waiting a few feet away on the opposite sidewalk; I wasn't sorry to avoid meeting with your patron and to miss whatever unpleasant things he would surely have to say to me, beginning with the debt of three hundred lire contracted by *our father*. As I waited I was thinking that in all the time we were together we hadn't spoken of our father, or only in passing, as though for you our father *didn't exist;* or about the girl either, about Giuliana, you hadn't said a word that showed you were worried about what might have happened to her, as if even she, for you, had never existed. Then I thought that certain recesses of your soul were still a mystery to me. After half an hour of waiting, I went away.

23

The visitors' parlor of the old folks home was a dark room on the first floor that looked out on a courtyard where the women residents walked around in their uniforms: a dress of gray material with a black apron tight across their hips.

The custodian knew all the visitors; as soon as they entered she would shout out a name in the direction of the courtyard.

"Casati!" she would say and soon after grandmother would appear.

She was still in good health, but a little unsteady on her legs; because of the step between the courtyard and the parlor she had to lean carefully on the door frame to cross the threshold. She was always neat and clean; I said I had never seen her so elegant. "We have inspection twice a day. And a bath once a week. We could get pneumonia!" She complained most of all about this. "They treat us like babies!" she said.

The parlor was full of people; a subdued, continual murmur of voices. Above the heads of the relatives the inmates watched one another, searching each other out with a look. One of them said to grandmother: "You see who came! And you were worried!"

"He came from Rome just to see me!"

"This is my daughter-in-law. She has brought me a dozen eggs," said the other, "and a little bit of butter."

("Her daughter-in-law has her own life," grandmother told me in a low voice. "She comes to see her every time a pope dies.")

"Hug your grandson! Is he the oldest?"

"Yes, he came from Rome just to see me. That is your son?"

"He's the middle one. The other one has to work."

("She has three sons and they keep her here," grandmother said. "It wouldn't have happened to me if your mother were alive.")

And the other woman: "Your grandson doesn't look as good as he did the last time."

"He works too hard!" replied grandmother. "And then the trip tired him." And to me: "You really are paler than usual...."

"I'm all right, I swear," I told her. "And you?"

"How do you think I am? A prisoner!"

The room was dark, with low ceilings; we were sitting opposite each other on straw-covered stools, holding hands — hers were always cold. We sat in silence for a long time, caressing each other's hands; I lowered my eyes and felt the looks over my head, like a rebuke and like a benediction. The whispering went on without interruption, a bell rang in the courtyard, a sister appeared in the doorway and disappeared.

"She is Sister Clementina, our policeman. But so good!" She let's me keep the chamber pot all night," grandmother said.

"Is the food still skimpy?"

"It's skimpy at night. They give us a cup of milk and coffee, but it's hot water. At times a plate of mashed potatoes."

"Is it good?"

"It stays in the stomach. I do without. You know that I hardly ever ate supper at home."

"Do you still go out once a week?"

"You want me to stay locked up here? If I don't go to see someone, at least I can get a little air."

She rearranged my sweater around my neck, with the anxious gesture of a mother, a lover.

That Thursday you arrived like you had promised me you would, and grandmother was beside herself with joy at having both of us with her. She took our hands and held them in her own, sniffing to keep from crying. You were a little embarrassed and looked around to regain your composure.

"Casati! Today you have both of them!"

"My daughter has sent them to me! The oldest came from Rome just to see me!"

You said, "Grandmother, don't answer them!" It was a reprimand, and grandmother apologized. She stroked your hair. You addressed her formally, as *your father* had you do as a boy.

"These women say that I'll wear you out by looking at you so much.... When you leave here watch out for the automobiles. And be careful when you go by Piazza Signoria: it's always windy there. Go by Via Condotta!"

Then I said: "Grandmother, we'll all three be together for Easter, are you glad? Easter's in two weeks. We'll go eat in a restaurant."

"But will his patron allow it?" she said, and her voice trembled. She added, "Let's meet in the afternoon instead. I'm invited to Semira's. Come get me there."

"*My father* will allow it, if you don't mind," you said. Grandmother made the gesture of a child. She passed her finger under her nose to control her emotion. She brought our heads closer to each other, kissed us on the forehead, first you, then me. She left a touch of saliva at my hairline.

I said: "Go to Semira and cancel the invitation. We'll come get you at noon." She protested again, weakly, then said: "When have you ever obeyed me!"

24

It was late afternoon, well into March, and the warmth of springtime was in the air. On the facade of the old folks home the ivy seemed greener. Coming out from the dark parlor made the light of the sunset flowing over the houses blinding. We seemed to be coming out of a prison, and it made me sad; I made fists inside the pockets of my overcoat. I took hold of your arm. You looked around you, absentmindedly, and it seemed to me my hand was weighing on you. Then I asked, "How was it?"

"All settled!" you looked around again. The sky was all pink and white low on the horizon; the red disk of the sun was behind the buildings reflecting its light on the highest windows.

We walked a long time in silence, instinctively turning onto Via Condotta as grandmother had advised. You offered to buy a cup of chocolate at the "Bar Fiorenza." The shops on Via de' Calzaiuoli were lighted, the evening traffic was thick in the center of the city. You sipped your chocolate and suddenly, between one sip and another, you said: *"My father* wants to talk to you."

"Right now?" I asked you.

"Yes, it's better. There's nothing new, but we should give him this satisfaction."

He was waiting for us in the rented room where he had reconstructed a piece of Villa Rossa. Hanging on the wall was the portrait of the baron and the three prints of a fox hunt; I recognized the carved wooden beds, even the chairs and table — all furniture that had once been in your private rooms on San Leonardo. This was a more comfortable room, with dark walls, where everything was in its place — a "chapel," I thought; an atmosphere lurked there of old houses where the inhabitants had placed a remembrance in every square centimeter; and they fed on these memories, lived off them. Rather, they did not live, but slowly prepared to die. And there was the ancient dimension of silence that I had forgotten about.

Upon entering I said "good evening" in a low voice, as one speaks to the person next to him in a church. Your patron, in a dressing gown, said, "Here's the rascal!" He had his old laugh, though a little more cordial now. He offered me a chair. We sat around the table.

First he asked me for details of my life, and smiled at my vagueness, showing his opaque teeth, his ivory-colored face: a leather hide weathered by time. At last he said, "And so you should be a good example for your brother...."

It grew dark; you turned on the light on your dresser, and in that half-light he carried on. He spoke in a calm tone veiled in irony that offended me at first; then I became more tolerant. I thought of other things while I listened to him, I thought of my evening as soon as I got away from there. He retold the story of your adoption; what he had done for you: he enumerated the sacrifices, the "three hundred lire," the indifference our family had shown for your future.

Then he said, "I'm not reproaching Ferruccio at all. If I could go back I'd do everything the same way. But now I can't do anything. Now I am old, without work, living on the last of my savings. I take bread from my mouth to keep him in school, and he allows himself the luxury of failing. I've done everything to give him an education, and he plays the gallant with the first little trollop he meets. I'll say this to you also: either Ferruccio gets his head straight or I'll send him back to his father. He'll see what it means! And if he fails this year I'll send him to work!"

You listened contritely, as one listens to a boring lecture when the professor is watching — without any expression. He talked away in his calm tone, alternating sarcastic sniggers with hand gestures.

"See what we have come to?" he said to me, indicating the room. "None of this means anything to him. It's as though it didn't concern him. He thinks I am immortal, and that for all his life there will be hot water and breakfast when he wakes up. He'll find out when I send him to work!" He pronounced "when I send him to work" like someone threatening a torture he knew how to carry out.

Then he said: "It's obvious Ferruccio has taken after his mother.... But he has to overcome it!"

I shook myself out of the lethargy I was lost in; I felt flushed and said, "What's that?"

"Never mind, it's too delicate a subject," your patron said.

I was hardly able to keep from jumping up from the chair and grabbing him by the lapels of his dressing gown; I suppressed the cry inside me. I stayed in my seat and remembered your words in the automobile. I had only the strength to say, in a cultured and ridiculous tone, "Allow me to say that as far as mama is concerned you are badly informed!"

"You are right to defend her," he replied. "But let's forget it."

At that point I got up to leave.

25

During that night we had spent together, when you had asked me how I managed to get along, I didn't tell you that from time to time I made money doing research in the library for friends who were university students. That is how I got money in those days.

You were punctual and together we went to pick up grandmother at Semira's — an old family friend who lived on Viale Petrarca, between Porta San Frediano and Porta Romana.

I only said to you, "Was it all right with *your father* for you to come?" I was waiting for you to

say something about my visit, but you answered
"yes" and nothing more.

"Where do you think we should take
grandmother?" I asked. "What do you think about
'Oreste'?"

"Doesn't that seem too elegant?"

"'Pennello'?"

"I don't know."

"Think a second-class restaurant would be
better? I have money, you know."

"That's not it."

"What about 'Ceviosa'?"

"I think an out-of-the-way restaurant would be
better."

We were both thinking the same thing and didn't
have the courage to say it. I was insistent; "Why
out-of-the-way? We mustn't tire her."

"We can take a streetcar. It's her clothes.
Everyone will recognize her as being from the old
folks home."

I felt extremely sad, depressed, like someone
who has given up and can be neither humiliated nor
offended. We walked through the working man's
area. It was Easter Sunday and Piazza del Carmine
was swarming with people going to mass. The
food shops had big displays in their windows, but
the butchers' shops looked as though they had been
plundered of all their meat; in the delicatessens
chicken and game were turning slowly on large
spits; the pastry shops were more crowded than
usual. It was clear that even the most restricted
domestic budgets were being stretched this once
to celebrate the solemn occasion. And the people
also, poorly dressed and vociferous, unconsciously
moderated their actions with an unusual levity.

Nearly all the doorsteps of the houses had been scrubbed and only a few clothes hung from windows. Some men were seated outside an inn playing cards. As we passed by one of them shouted: "Admit you have the aces and threes, son of a.... I promised my wife I wouldn't swear before eating the blessed egg!" Further on, a young boy asked us for a light for his cigarette; he winked and said, "For Easter!" Everyone was in the same mood, not hypocritically devout, but unconsciously seeking comfort in their dearest loves, as though testing their consistency — a feeling that went beyond the occasion that was almost forgotten. The contentment of having a family and feeling protected by it was obvious in every face.

You walked by my side, elegant and serious, watching where you put your feet on the uneven pavement covered here and there by garbage, paper, horse dung, until we reached the clean, straight Viale, with its trees beginning to leaf.

Your silence didn't encourage me to share my thoughts with you. "Are you happy to be spending Easter with me and grandmother?" And then I added, "It's the first Easter you've spent with the family!"

You looked at me a little surprised, smiled weakly, and said, "Why didn't we go to *our father's*? That would have avoided all the complications."

"Our father invited us, in fact. But I turned it down because I thought you might be uncomfortable."

"Uhm, uhm!" was all you said.

26

Semira's daughter opened the door, and the whole family welcomed us and offered us a homemade liqueur. They immediately invited us to eat with them, but I stubbornly refused, seeing that you would have been pleased to accept, "in order to avoid all the complications."

"Isn't grandmother here yet?"

"She's in the other room. She's coming now," they told us.

"Here's your grandmother!" Semira said, leading the way from the kitchen.

When grandmother came into the room she seemed like another person. She was wearing a green dress of a material like brocade, and over her shoulders a jacket with a black velvet collar. Her skirt was full, reaching down to her calves; her shoes were black silk. A black silk shawl hung from her neck like a stole. She had combed her hair into a bun; her ears were half covered by two long black earrings edged with gold. With her hands joined she proceeded a little hesitantly, like a child going toward the altar for her first communion; her face expressed the same joy and excitement.

"Your grandmother has gotten all dressed up," said Semira. "Here are her boyfriends. She can't wait to smother them with kisses."

You and I went to her at the same instant, and she gathered us both in her arms. Then turning to these people, she said: "In my whole life I've never enjoyed them together."

As I stroked her arm I recognized her dress: I had seen her wear it a few times before, on special occasions. And these, after our mother's death, were rare to non-existent. You smilingly tolerated her caresses. I said to her, "You really look nice, grandmother. Like a real lady!"

"You see," said Semira. "Like a lady. The one who said that knows what he's talking about."

"It's good material," grandmother said. "Your mother made it for me a few months before she died. I've probably worn it ten times. It's the only thing I have left. When I die you must dress me in it, don't forget. Semira will have it."

Grandmother was sure that we would accept the invitation; she didn't want to go out dressed up like that. "If someone from inside there sees me and tells on me they'll take away my permission to go out for three months and they'll put me on the people-to-be-watched list. Sister Clementina will take away my chamber pot. It's too big a risk to take."

But I was insistent, and by now even you were, too. "We'll be careful. We'll hide you between us." And Semira said, "To keep asking you to stay now would only be a nuisance, it seems to me. Besides, Rosa, who is going to recognize you? You seem like another person!"

"We'll take a carriage," I said.

But grandmother said no, as obstinate as a little girl who capriciously wants to deny herself a vacation that would fill her with joy. I came close to her and whispered in her ear: "We'll be freer, we three alone. And besides, Ferruccio isn't comfortable with these people."

"It would be cheaper, though," she said.

I understood that she was surrendering.

27

At Porta Romana there were no carriages, so we decided to take a taxi. Grandmother refused. "Where do you want to go? To 'Oreste'? You're crazy. They'll have us by the neck."

You were smiling. There was a condescension in your attitude toward grandmother; I wasn't sure whether it was motivated by affection or insolence. "Where would you like to go?" I asked her.

"Some place inexpensive." Her every gesture, her every word, were the indication of a contentment that she refused in order to enjoy it more.

"Why don't we go to the country?" I asked.

We made her get into a taxi. It reached Via Senese in a hurry, and in a few minutes we were in the hills. Grandmother sat between us, numb with happiness: "It's the first time I've been in a private automobile! Oh! We're already on Due Strade. It's been years since I've been here! Have we already passed Via del Gelsomino?"

You and I were sitting on the edge of the folding seat to give her more room. "I feel like I'm on a merry-go-round," she said. "Who knows what it will cost!"

Then you said: "Why worry about the expense? Just enjoy yourself!"

"My boy, money costs perspiration. You're lucky you don't know what that means!"

You darkened at her reply and she noticed it. She put a hand on your thigh: "I didn't mean to hurt you."

We had gone beyond the toll walls; the street was jammed with automobiles and carts, and the taxi had to go behind a streetcar at a walking pace. A wall on our right with willow and cypress trees rising above it caught grandmother's attention.

"That's the Allori cemetery," she said, turning toward you. "The baron's tomb is there, isn't it?"

You turned your face toward the window, instinctively removing your hat. Now the taxi had picked up speed, and soon we were at the outskirts of Galluzzo, which seemed like an abandoned town.

"Everyone is eating their turkey," I said. "Pretty soon it will be our turn."

"But the others are together with their families, and we're out like some foreigners," she said, resting her head against the back of the seat with her eyes half closed.

The taxi slowed down to cross Ema bridge, and when it was on the road again we saw the flight of steps on our left leading to Certosa.

You said, "We're already at Certosa, grandmother. Do you like the liqueur the brothers make?"

It was a way of distracting her. There was an affectionate tone in your words. We looked at each other over her head, exchanging a warm, encouraging look of understanding, as though at the bedside of a sick person saved from death.

Grandmother roused herself to answer you. "I know that recipe, too. I could make it just as good!"

On our left, behind the low wall, fields sloped down toward the Ema that made an elbow turn and then disappeared into the distance where a scattering of factory buildings and farm houses stood among the olive and cypress trees. The taxi stopped in front of a country house. In tall letters along the entire front of the place was written "TRATTORIA AI BOTTAI WITH GARDEN — WINE AND OIL" and lower down, on the side toward the country, in calligraphy: *The plow tills the soil, but the sword defends it.*

Grandmother said, "Let's not fuss. Let the taxi go and we'll go back by streetcar."

We entered by way of the "garden:" an open space enclosed by green walls and bordered in the rear by a brick balustrade, below which ran the Ema. The tables were set, some people were eating and laughing. Their words and laughter had a particular sound in the clear, sun-bathed atmosphere, as if they remained suspended in the air waiting for an echo that didn't come. The woman who had shown us the way from the entrance said, "Will you eat outside or in the dining room?"

"It's better in the dining room," I said. "It's still cool outside."

The dining room was at the end of the garden, with two large windows with panes like a greenhouse, overlooking the river. We sat down at a table near one of the windows, a little removed from the other three or four tables where some other people were eating and laughing. And for the whole time it was as though we were alone —you, I, and our grandmother.

28

It had rained for several days and the Ema carried these last rains of winter within the tumultuous confines of its river bed. At night the water had overflowed the banks, going as far as the first clods in the fields. Opposite us, several meters beyond the river, was a mill with its immobile water wheel, and next to it was a farmhouse on whose facade was written: *This is the war we prefer.* The farm animals were grazing almost to the banks, where a pig wallowed in the mud. Then a girl appeared in the only window in the house and began to sing. Through the half-open dining-room windows came the words of an old song:

> *Tabarin, tu sei il mio regno d'or*
> *o per te io sono il re di cuori;*
> *ma di un cuor che veramente amavo,*
> *sono lo schiavo, ahimè, e mi si crede un re....*

> Tabarin, you are my golden kingdom
> oh for you I am the king of hearts;
> but of the heart I truly loved,
> I am a slave, alas, and I think I am a king....

"O fool!" said grandmother. We laughed. Among the three of us grandmother was the youngest. You were red-cheeked, relaxed, and happier than I had ever seen you. Grandmother said we had eaten like kings, and she resisted all our urging to take another piece of chicken or fruit. She even refused another drop of wine.

"On special occasions like these, Sister Clementina stops each one of us to ask how we have spent our holiday, but it's really just an excuse to smell our breath. If she notices we've been drinking, there's trouble!"

You were a little excited and said recklessly, "She could take away your chamber pot, eh?" You reddened and gave me an alarmed look. "Excuse me, grandmother," you added.

But grandmother answered calmly, "What do you think? When I know it's under the bed I never use it. But if I don't have it I have to get up three or four times. The bathroom is at the end of the dormitory and there's always a draft in the hall."

Every once in a while she would ask what time it was, and you would tell her, "It's two o'clock, two-thirty, two forty-five."

"Watch the time. When it's four we have to get moving. The streetcar will take some time, then I have to change my clothes at Semira's, and by six I have to be back inside. We'll have only ten minutes to spare. If we get back late we can't have permission to leave for another two weeks the first time and an additional two weeks every other time we're late. After five or six times we have to leave. We're like soldiers."

"But you'll never have to fight a war," I said — I, the careless one this time.

"Do you think it's not like fighting a war, being in there?" she sighed. Then she squeezed my arm and her face became thoughtful. "Is it true there's going to be a war?"

"No, no," you and I said together.

"It seems that those who want to volunteer to go to Africa are registering in secret. The son of one of the women in the home has registered for it. His fiancée came crying to his mother to make him change his mind."

"Those are all stories."

"Even Sister Clementina says it's not true!"

You smiled at her, saying, "Read what's written on that house."

"What is it?"

"Don't you see it?"

"Grandmother doesn't know how to read," I said.

"It says: 'This is the war we prefer.'"

"Which means?"

"That we prefer to work in the fields," you said.

"I wish that were true!" Then she said, "Are you a member of the Fascist Youth?"

"How can we be at our age?" I asked her.

"I'm in the group for older boys," you said. "Those with the white braid on the uniform. Have you seen them?"

"Bravo!" she said, then she added: "Your grandfather would certainly have had a fit if he had seen you dressed like that." She leaned over the table and whispered, "He wouldn't have agreed with these times. He couldn't hurt a fly. He would go around the block in order not to have to take off his hat when a Fascist parade came by. I worried when he didn't come right home."

Then she asked you, "Do you remember him?"

"No."

"He came to see you a couple of times at Villa Rossa. You were too young to remember him. He died in 1925. The first of May. He knew he was dying and he wanted to be kept alive by injections until the next day, the first of May. 'If I die on the first of May, and there's a Heaven, I'm sure I'll go there,' he said. When it was one hour past midnight he found the strength to sit up in bed and begin singing a song, then he began the death struggle."

"Why did he want to die on the first of May?"
you asked.

And she replied: "The first of May was the day
we were married."

29

Grandmother sat at the head of the table, her arms
on the tablecloth; we sat at the sides. The girl was
leaning on the windowsill and had stopped singing.
At the other tables they were still eating, talking,
and laughing, but we had turned our backs to the
wall and it was as though we were alone in front of
the mill on the horizon, with a backdrop of intense
blue sky and that girl at the windowsill.

"What time is it?" asked grandmother.

"Five minutes after three."

"Let's not let it get past four o'clock."

Then she said, "War is a terrible thing. If it
hadn't been for the war your mother would still be
here with us. In fact, we would all be together in
our house, and she would have made the pancakes."

"You've never told me about the pancakes," I
said.

"What do you mean I've never told you! It was
her passion. She went into the kitchen only when it
was time to make pancakes. She did everything by
herself and didn't want me to help her. She mixed
the chestnut flour with water in a bowl and then
fried it. Before she put it on the table she would
have eaten half of it! God forgive me, how many
times I scolded her for using so much olive oil!"

"When you scolded her what did she say?"

"She never answered me back, she never showed me any disrespect as long as she lived.... And if there wasn't any oil she would take two or three thimbles, fill them with the flour and cook them under the ashes made by the wood burning in the kitchen stove. That is a country custom I taught her when she was a little girl!"

You and I listened carefully to her; I recognized my same desire in your attentive look.

"Talk, grandmother, talk."

"Eh, yes, the damned war. If there had been no war there would have been no Spanish influenza."

"What was that?" you asked.

"It was an epidemic that struck us toward the end of the war. Our mother died from it; didn't you know that?"

You made a face and smiled a little bitterly; it seemed that you thought grandmother and I were making fun of you. Your face assumed a suspicious expression.

"Talk, grandmother."

"What time is it? Ask for the bill, anyway. It will save time."

"Talk about mama."

"I think she would be happy to have you near her, now that you are grown!"

"Did mama go to school?" you asked her.

"Certainly, to all the elementary levels."

"Only the elementary?"

"Why not? If you're going to be a dressmaker!"

Then a thought came to mind that I had never had before. "When she came home from work, did mama read? Did she have any books?"

"Yes, she would often bring a book home. I think the workers at the dressmaker's shop would

lend them to each other. But after she got married
she stopped. When your father was called up for
the war, she started again."

"What books were they?" I said, careless again.

"I don't know. They could have been books
about love. But it was hard for her to concentrate.
She always came home with a headache.... What
time is it?"

"We'll go now, don't worry."

You clapped your hands to ask for the bill. The
girl had disappeared from the window; on the other
side of the river two boys with an empty jar were
searching the ground, for earthworms, perhaps.

30

We went back to Semira's house where grandmother put on her prisoner's clothes again; you left
us because *your father* wanted you to meet him at
five o'clock. I went with grandmother as far as the
entrance to the old folks home.

I was happy to have her on my arm, now more
than ever, now that she was wearing the clothes
from the home and I had conquered my shame. (I
had had a bad moment when we were presented
with the check; it left me with just enough to pay
the return fare on the streetcar.)

As we came nearer the home my happiness
gradually turned to melancholy; it was already
evening and the streets were crowded with people,
the movie houses had emptied, and the cafes were
full — there wasn't an empty chair at the outside
tables. Grandmother had put a black scarf on her

head, tight under her chin. Her gray tunic dress came nearly to her shoes, and the black shawl on her shoulders was fastened with a safety pin. All the many years of her life returned to her in these clothes. The intense activity and emotion of the day had fatigued her; only in her eyes was a light still shining.

"What do you think of Ferruccio?" I asked her.

"...he has really grown! Even though you are far away don't abandon him. He is your brother and you are all he has.... Are you really leaving tomorrow?"

"Yes, but I'll be back soon. We'll have more days like this."

"I'm happy with things the way they are. It's enough that you have your health and get along with each other."

We had reached Via dell'Anguillare, now immersed in shadow. Grandmother stopped, dug in the pocket of her gray tunic, and pulling out a closed fist, said, "Take this. You spent a lot today and now you have your trip back...."

I struggled lightly with her. She pleaded with me: "I don't have any use for this, really. Besides, it's the same fifty lire you gave me for Christmas. I've never had any need for it! As soon as you reach Rome you can send it back to me, if there's any left."

"But you should use it. You could get something hot in the evening; didn't you tell me you had a canteen?"

"Yes, but you know someone always helps me; those ladies I worked for, Semira.... Believe me, they don't allow me to go without a thing. Take it. I won't sleep thinking that you could use it on your trip. Let me see what money you have. If you have enough I won't insist, but one never has enough for a train trip!"

"All right," I said. "When I get there I'll send you a money order."

"Yes. Now for the first time you do what I say."

We were on the street of the home and from every intersection appeared men and women dressed in uniform. The men wore a rough black overcoat and a cap with a visor. The coat of arms of the Pio Istituto was displayed on the back of the overcoat. On the two sidewalks opposite each other filed the black and gray shapes of the inmates, a slow procession of abandoned old people. Grandmother wanted us to say our good-byes a little before the entrance. She was crying now.

"This could be the last time we see each other," she said. She kissed me on both cheeks, and in order to control her emotion she turned away abruptly; moving as quickly as she could, she entered the big door without looking back. I stood looking at her. I realized I had her fifty lire in my hand.

I walked toward the center of town and went down into the billiard room where we had met a month before. From the ping-pong room came a din of voices and shouts. I pushed open the door out of curiosity and immediately saw you, red-faced, surrounded by your excited friends. You managed to push your way through and came toward me. "If you don't mind," you said, stammering and holding back your anger. "If you don't mind, could you give me a loan? These swine," you added.

I gave you grandmother's fifty lire. It was enough; the bets weren't high in the kindergarten.

31

It was spring. The Arno returned to its slow rippling flow. The water was so clear you could see yourself by leaning over the embankment; the plane trees on the hills had their new leaves; the poor people of Santa Croce and San Frediano threw open the windows of their houses in the morning, as though they had stopped breathing during the winter to better protect themselves from the damp and cold. I stood at the window of my room gulping the air. My lungs never seemed full enough of air. The owner of the milk bar was wearing a flowery dress with short sleeves. She was also spring — and she agreed to come to my place. I worked all morning to make my room clean and neat. When she came in she said, "You have a great bachelor's apartment." She was young and beautiful; in the frame of the window the spring sky changed color a thousand times that afternoon.

At a certain point she said, "Did you know that your brother is courting me? He comes in the milk bar every day, sits at a table and orders a chocolate. He says nothing in particular to me, just follows me with his eyes. I pretend not to notice but can't help laughing. When I try to start a conversation, he won't join in. Before leaving he always says, 'If you don't mind, I'd rather my brother didn't know I came here!' He's very different from you. And yet you resemble one another. I couldn't say why, because you are two different types, and yet you can tell you're brothers."

"He had a different upbringing."

"He told me he goes to the university."

I laughed inwardly, asking her, "What impression did he make on you?"

"Must I be honest? He seems like a fragile person, someone who has never had anyone close to him that he could trust. I think he could torment himself over nothing. He is shy and touchy to an extreme. He must be unhappy, or am I wrong?"

"I think not," I said to her.

She said, "Perhaps your mother died when he was very young."

32

One evening during that April, 1935, I was caught in a downpour. As soon as I got home I fell into a deep sleep. I awoke with a heavy feeling in my chest, hardly able to breathe. I went over to open the window and the fresh morning air went down through my throat like a hammer blow. The taste of blood was in my mouth. A few hours later I was lying in a hospital bed. Two days passed and a friend visiting me there said the doctors had given me up for dead.

"They said you had been sick for too long without knowing it. What'll we do? Are you going to get up and leave, or do we admit that they were right?"

I told him, "Listen. I could throw everything in the lake — them and their x-rays. It's a question of getting my stomach back to normal."

We talked like that, but both of us, for different reasons, were frightened. He asked me, "Do you want me to notify someone?"

"No," I said. "Just have my brother come. You'll find him in the kindergarten."

Your face was paler than mine when you came to my bedside. I said to you, "If you don't mind, I can do without dying."

You tried to smile, but you couldn't finish a sentence. Your blue eyes avoided mine; sitting on a chair alongside the bed, your hands rested on your knees.

"Are you in a hurry?" I asked. You quickly said no. There was more affection in your silence than if you had clung to my neck sobbing. I looked at you, impressing your image inside of me, as though swallowing you; you were a sweet, cool thing that gave me relief. I had a very high fever — and I thought mama would be happy to have your picture. I might, in the end, open up my chest like one opens a cabinet —it would free me from the burning I was suffering —and mama could see your portrait, which I had incised there.

I spent two years in the sanitarium, among mountains and a lake. We wrote often. You had to quit your studies and were working as a clerk. Your letters were just like you: timid, shy, fearful of showing your feelings, yet bursting with affection and generosity. In them I recognized *one of the things that attached me to life*. One of the essentials.

Part Three

33

In Rome, one evening toward the end of 1944, I was called to the telephone. I heard your voice at the other end. "I just arrived. I'm in Piazza Risorgimento."

"How are you?"

"So so. But I'm able to walk, don't worry. I'll meet you in the bar."

We hadn't seen each other since September the year before; I had had to leave quickly, without even saying good-bye. I had left you seriously ill, and you were still not well. For several months I had had no news from you. After the liberation of Florence, one of your letters said you had spent almost all that year in the hospital.

I got on my bicycle to go meet you. It was already evening and the streets were dark and crowded, but the air was still warm and the wind on my face made me happy. That is the last hour of happiness I remember. I'll never again find the happy disposition of spirit that cheered that evening. One can become accustomed to persecution, executions, massacres; man is like a tree and after each one of his winters spring comes bringing new leaves and new vigor. The heart of man is a precise mechanism, complete with a few essential levers to withstand cold, hunger, injustice, cruelty, betrayal; but destiny can wound him like a child tears off a butterfly wing. His heart comes out of it with a tired beat; from then on perhaps the person will become better, perhaps stronger, and perhaps more decisive and aware in his work, but he will never again find that fullness of life and humor in his spirit that touched happiness. That evening was the 18th of December 1944.

The bar was deserted. You were sitting at a table by the window; on the corner a foreign soldier and a girl were embracing. You stood up when I came in. You were tall, transparent, your blond two days' growth of beard shadowed your face like a soft light. The look on your face was sweet, uncertain, almost veiled.

"Let me see you," I said and looked into your eyes that were, as in every innocent, your mirror. There was the sign of a hard struggle in them, and in the intensity of their aquamarine color, a firmness stronger than evil.

Because there was no streetcar or taxi you sat on the bicycle bar; we balanced your suitcase on the handlebars and rode slowly into the city. Everything can now become a symbol. As your height made it impossible for me to see the street, I pedaled and *you guided me.* I barely pedaled, just fast enough to keep my balance, to avoid hitting something. Coasting, we entered Via Tomacelli where the traffic became heavier; you amused yourself by ringing the bell and calling out to those we passed. You asked me the name of the streets, the news of the past year. You said, "I seem to be in a new world." And then, "Let's hope Rome brings me good luck."

We slept in the same bed, just as we had many years before. We talked until dawn. You said, "Do you remember? Ten years ago you were ill and I was well."

"You'll get well, too," I replied.

"How much has happened in the past ten years!"

We were in bed; the room faced the courtyard; we could hear scraping from the floor above us every once in awhile, and the echo of a shot would come from far away. You turned toward me, lying on your side. "We've changed a lot in these ten years. Me particularly, but you, too." You leaned over my face and kissed me.

We remembered the ten years during which we had learned to love each other.

34

On my return after the two years I had spent in the sanitarium, you were unemployed. They had let you go from an office because of "lack of funds." You had already experienced the daily contact with a hostile world and the daily sacrifices poor people are forced to make. It was obvious you had undergone a shock from which you were only now recovering. You were discovering yourself. You were realizing, painfully, that up to then you had lived a precarious and absurd life, completely opposite from the reality you must now face without the means to do so. When you finally *discovered the world with your own eyes,* it was no longer the world that was externally familiar to you, but another, different and hostile, where you had to make your own way, and where your habits, customs, and your own thoughts were unsuitable and particularly detrimental. The new reality rejected you. Your patron had moved another step toward absolute poverty, and the harshness of his criticism, as well-meaning as it was, did not help you overcome the obstacles, although it led you to face them impetuously, committing yourself to a series of failures.

You said, "They were right to fire me. I don't know how to do anything. I can't type or keep books; I don't know how to write a business letter. I need to learn something. But I don't have time to learn anything when I have to earn a living.... It's a vicious circle."

You had the persistence to follow job announcements in the newspapers for weeks and months: for a management-level position they asked you for references you couldn't provide, and if you applied for the job of errand boy they always preferred someone else because he had a bicycle. Snow fell the winter of 1937. You noticed it at daybreak and went out to earn a few lire as a snow-shoveler, but a crowd of unemployed men were ahead of you. You worked as a salesman for a heraldic office: you knocked on doors and tried to convince housewives to buy the parchment that attributes illustrious ancestors to every family. At each door suspiciously closed in your face, many pounding heart beats. In one month you earned thirty lire! During the population census you were hired to deliver forms to homes. With your first pay you invited me to supper at Beccatelli.

You opened your eyes to this reality, but there was nothing in your preceding life to help you face it. Even that careful grooming you still had, and which made you always seem distinctive and impeccable, inspired uneasiness; it denied you the minimal, disinterested, help that anyone might have wanted to give you. "I would like to do something," our mutual friends would tell me, "but I'm afraid I might offend him with so little!"

You couldn't find any way to get a foothold; you lacked that faith that comes to a man — and you were already twenty years old — from the society that has seen him grow up, where he always lived, and in virtue of which he feels surrounded by a collective solidarity, or even by an aversion that is itself an incentive to struggle for bread. Instead you were excluded, outside the circle. With the experience of life at Villa Rossa, following the example of your patron, you avoided even saying hello in order not to have to suffer the offense of their pity. You even avoided your former school friends. In your eyes they represented the image of your unsuccessful life; towards them you had mixed feelings of nostalgia, childish shame, envy, and above all a sense of separation, an excessive and mistaken life-long regard for the cultured and privileged classes that led you to what has been, in varying degrees, your enormous, understandable, pathetic, dramatic inferiority complex.

You lived in a kind of moral prison that you tried to escape day by day by scratching the walls of convention and inhibition that the past had put up around you. Your spirit had undergone a trauma too violent, making each day a series of difficult struggles that invariably left you wounded. Your sensitivity led you to view even the most banal and fortuitous conflict as a deep blow, extracting from it every variety of humiliation and discomfort. I know now that you were defenseless, devoted to a sterile sacrifice, in a world where even the lamb is constrained to fiercely defend his own innocence.

How many recommendations were needed for you to become an office boy for a low-level government office! You did the cleaning, lit the stoves, went on errands, printed the letters on the copying machine. During the evenings, in the deserted offices, you learned how to type, you were initiating yourself into the mysteries of bureaucracy. You were promised a promotion to clerk as soon as possible. (You were dismissed from military service because of a heart defect: that grieved you like a prison sentence.)

35

You were in love. She was sixteen years old, small, plump, loquacious, with black curls and surprisingly shrewd and laughing eyes. With Sicilian parents, but born in Florence, she spoke our dialect in such a clear sweet voice that everyone liked her immediately. She was, like you, a simple, open creature, but nevertheless driven by a will that didn't wither before obstacles. You spent your happiest days with her. You were two adolescents barely blossoming, and for whom sin did not yet exist, but only a spiritual communion like spring in the meadows when the wind caresses the grass and there is the smell and taste of air and light. Her name was Enzina, and she could have been your wife.

One day I was in the hills at a friend's house, looking out of the window when I saw you two walking down the path. You were holding her by the arm; she was like a baby that you were trying to rock. You just managed, mussing your curls, to lift her the height of your shoulders. She had a bunch of lilacs in her hand which you wanted to get away from her. You struggled, holding each other tight, in love. She got loose and ran ahead; you both ran around a tree. The path was deserted and your voices filled the air. I shouted from the window, "Fine thing!" You stopped like a balking horse, flaming red, and said, "Oh!" almost as though I were a ghost.

Enzina raising her sly face, said, "We can do what we want!"

"That's my brother," you told her.

"Oh, dear!" she said and ran away, her own laughter following her.

You ran to her. The friend standing beside me at the window said, "They look like Mutt and Jeff." You both waved to me from a distance; she shook the bunch of lilacs.

36

That winter grandmother died.

It was on a Sunday with a frigid, gray sky and a wind on the streets that took away your breath. When we got there she looked already dead, her breath coming harsh and rapid. On the medical

record was written "Pneumonia." In her delirium
grandmother called out, "You saw sister take away
my chamber pot! Now I'll die, you saw her. She is
a good person, but she took my chamber pot, you
saw her!"

The infirmary, on the first floor like the parlor,
looked on the courtyard; through the window one
saw two trees with bare limbs that the wind
whistled through. From the other beds tired voices
complained from time to time. A sister sat at a
table at the end of the room. In the bed opposite
grandmother's was an old woman propped up on
pillows and wrapped in a shawl. She made a sign
for us to come to her.

"She's been going on like that. The other
women resented it because Casati had a chamber
pot and they didn't. Then sister took it from her.
Casati had to get up at night and took sick. Now
she is raving, but that's what she wants to say!"

The old woman took us both by the arm, and
almost in our ears said, "My dears! How one goes
down within these walls! I had children. I have a
son in America, and another that died in the war...."

You looked at the old woman talking to us, your
eyes open wide, frightened. You said to her,
"Thank you, signora," shaking her hand as you left
her bedside.

Grandmother lay still, her head sunk in pillows
and her arms abandoned outside the blankets. She
was calling mama in her delirium: "Now that the
babies are alone what can I do?" Her eyes were
always closed, her lips barely moving, tormented
by thirst. Her face, without any expression to
illuminate it, was thin and withered, with the skin
smooth at the temples and brow where the pallor of

death was falling. She was an old, tired creature who trusted in death as a longed-for rest; only her words, spoken with difficulty, told us that her spirit was still near us.

You didn't take your eyes from her face for a moment; you were a statue staring in anguish at grandmother in her agony. She had some moments of lucidity; she recognized us, she held our hands within hers. Tears ran down her face; her hands were dry and cold and warm like snow that freezes and then melts. The next day we laid out her body in a walnut casket. Semira dressed her in her green dress, her long earrings, her silk scarf worn like a shawl.

The mortuary chapel was in the basement of the old folks home, in a completely bare room, perhaps once a cellar storeroom, with only a crucifix hanging on one wall. The bier was placed on the ground in the middle of the room. Grandmother had an almost smiling expression. You and I were alone with her, and there was no mystery around us, no presentiment of death. She almost smiled at us, giving us a long, affectionate farewell. Tears came as in a sweet, touching moment. Instinctively *we held hands.*

When grandmother had entered the infirmary she gave the sister all her money for safekeeping. It was twenty-four lire. We gave it to the custodian.

37

A thousand things reveal a man: his way of walking and doing things, how he chews his food, how he ties his shoes, the way he holds the paddle in a game of ping-pong, his sleeping position. A weakness, a satisfaction, a resentment, seem contradictory to us when the knowledge we have of the individual or that the individual has of himself is incomplete. In reality they are always logical and natural, just as a planted seed flourishes on good ground. Everything is useful for revealing a man to us: how he reacts in a disaster, how he approaches a prostitute.

One day I saw you in a house of prostitution. Before you could see me I hid among those waiting in the corridor. Every time the men heard the heavy step of a girl on the stairs above they looked at one another to get the courage to take the initiative when she appeared. The girls were half-nude, happy and patient as tame mules; they would go through the parlor to the desk where an older woman, with bleached hair and fingers covered with rings, sat. The girls went by and you sat quietly in a chair, with your hat in your hands — until you got up to leave. I wanted to get out ahead of you but was blocked in the hallway.

In the street you said to me: "How can you engage a girl by a nod of your head, without ever speaking a word! And that woman who counts the money like a shopkeeper."

"Then why go there?" I asked you.

"That's the first time, and I think it will be the last."

You were blinking your eyes as though the light was bothering you. "What beautiful girls! I'll never understand it!" You were serious, and you were twenty years old. We bought some chestnut cake from the vendor on Piazza San Piero; I noticed your hand was trembling.

"Are you cold?" I asked you.

"No, but I'm shaking all over. Excuse me. I shouldn't have tried to have this experience."

38

Then I moved from Florence. In its precipitous course your life gathered its final and deepest sorrows; at the same time you experienced your first and last happiness, just as a pale, dim sun appears for an instant before being attacked and extinguished by storm clouds.

Enzina left you; you fell in love with another girl, married her, a baby was born. Your promotion to clerk was always promised and always postponed. You and your wife suffered extreme hardships. She wasn't what you wanted; she wasn't — and she was not to blame — the "other half of you."

True love belongs to the poor. When a poor man and woman marry, they must become one in order to endure and give each other courage. To love one another is to give each other courage, protection, blood joined to blood, a kind of secret brotherhood. A poor man whose work brings only misery is stronger with a companion by his side. Only then, when the strength of his arms are fully valued, does he see clearly the meaning of his own existence on earth: his anxieties are drowned in a caress. But the love of the poor is more fragile: either the mosaic of souls fits together exactly or everything breaks into bits and scatters, and love becomes brutalization, desperation, hatred, and even tragedy. A poor man can make every error that his poverty prompts, can swear and get drunk, can also hate his work, can even, in a lost moment, steal. He will always find the energy to recover. But he is not allowed to make a mistake in his choice of a companion. This error freezes his heart, poisons his blood, takes away his future, since his only future was love. *You made this mistake.*

The roosters had already been crowing for a while when we fell asleep and the first streetcars ran on the boulevards.

39

We spent Christmas together. You had been in Rome only once before, on your honeymoon. You liked to walk along the river and to go down the steps of the Ripetta. It was Christmas, the dinner hour, and it seemed like we were the only two living in the city, on the river. You picked up a rock and threw it into the water, holding the lapel of your overcoat to protect yourself from the wind.

"When I'm well I'm going to live in Rome. I'll bring my wife and little girl here. My wife will like it, you'll see. And my little girl will grow up beside me. I haven't been with her since she was born. I've been in hospitals for two years."

There was a longing in your voice. "Today is Christmas," you said, "every family is together in a warm house. I've never had that. You'll laugh, but I believe in those things...."

I told you I believed in them, too, and I saw you smile to yourself; you were smiling and your blue eyes were calm, veiled in a melancholy that softened them; an immaterial yet visible shadow was on your face, like that of a man barely rested after long labor. I asked you what you were thinking.

"I was thinking — don't laugh — that in a few years my little girl will be leaving me a little Christmas letter under my plate on a day like this!"

After dinner in an inexpensive restaurant, we sat in a cafe waiting for the movie house to open.

"Let's talk about your illness," I said.

"The doctors don't know anything. It's all in the intestines. They can make the diagnosis, but they can't find the bacillus. When they discover that, the cure will be easy. They say it's not tuberculosis, it's not malaria, it's not an amoeba — who knows what the devil it is...."

You entered the hospital on Saint Stephen's Day; you were an interesting "case," and the doctors fell on you like flies on sugar, like pigs at the trough, like boxers in the last round. It was, for you, the last round.

Before taking a bath you undressed in my presence. You seemed like an athlete in your height; your legs were thin, full at the thighs; your head seemed more handsome above your nude chest. Only your unmuscular arms were surprising in their flabbiness. Your chest was covered with thick, soft, brown hair. I was deeply moved at the sight of you. I had to confess to myself that until that moment I had loved an arbitrary image of you, neither physical nor real — the image of a child, making me feel protective and indulgent. In my heart *you had not grown up until that moment*. It was a discovery that at first alarmed me, only to flood me immediately afterward with sweet fraternal pride.

40

With a case like yours, a doctor is like a storyteller in the grips of a character in which he indistinctly sees great historical importance. On the blank page the writer is prepared to give life to a ghost. He writes, "He was blond and had the eyes...." He marks out the eyes; a black line remains on the paper. "He was blond, tall, and open in his actions." It is still too unspecific, and the writer draws a line through the whole sentence. Now the page seems like a stabbed body. When the writer has filled the sheet of paper, the black lines have multiplied, the body is full of wounds, then the rejected words show through the cancellations like rivulets of clotted blood. To the doctor the character is a mysterious illness that he tries to control with the inks of his trade: remedies, operations, transfusions. He puts together his story, one line after the other, but this collection is a man's body that receives the stabs, and the wounds are real wounds, the blood is red, warm blood.

You entered the hospital stronger than I. The day before an old man was painfully pulling a cart over the curb on Viale Gorizia. The incline made his work twice as difficult; a poorly balanced box slipped and fell. The man stopped, and with great difficulty he managed to straighten the shaft, his face red from the effort, his neck strained. If he had slacked up on his effort the cart might have overturned and he could have broken his arm. I wanted to help him put the box back on the cart; it was a wooden crate, full of canned preserves. I tried but could barely get it off the ground. "Let me do it," you said. You squatted down, raised the crate with the help of your knees and with one swooping motion let it fall in place. The man thanked you, then said: "Now help me get it started." Your shoulders pushing against the loaded cart got it moving. ("Did you notice how much he resembled *our father,*" you said a little later.)

Now you were nailed to your bed. The first thing the doctors had written on your blank record was "Sulfonamide in strong doses."

I found you looking as if they had beaten you all over with a whip. You were uncomfortable in the bed, like a soldier in makeshift quarters. Because the bed was too short for your legs you had to keep your knees bent. The horsehair mattress was old and uneven, as though filled with rocks. Because the Germans had taken all the sheets, the hospital could provide only a lightweight blanket full of holes.

You said, "Sulfonamide and I are old friends. It works for a while. It's a kind of cocaine; the dose has to be constantly increased. Only you can't take too much or you'll get poisoned."

"Why didn't you tell them you've already tried it?"

"I did tell them, but doctors are touchy. They are doubting Thomases. And they study poor people like us. Let's hope they can solve my problem!"

You were pale, already physically beaten, but patient, trusting; your eyes shone like the sun on the sea. You said, "I know I'm in good hands. The head physician is a genius. He cured Big Head (Mussolini) of ulcers and an amoeba. Just imagine him on his white horse at the Gates of Alexandria with diarrhea!"

And so it seemed like the sulfonamide was doing you some good. You got out of bed, and I met you on the hospital lanes. You had begun smoking again. The days were warm in January that year, 1945. We walked along the hospital lanes, talking of the war, communism, Big Head who must have had frequent attacks of his old illness, and of the partisans who had cured him this time. Of friends who had died in the Resistance, and of others who were still suffering from the occupation and were certainly still fighting bravely.

You said, "I know I'm being selfish, but I can't think about these things for long. The only important thing to me is getting well. I want to be with my family again." This thought was your comfort and your obsession: my little girl, how is my little girl? And your wife: "I've written to her — why doesn't she answer? I can't sleep at night for thinking of her. I talk to the seriously ill people to distract myself...."

One day, to ease your anxiety a little, you wanted to tell me the story of yourself and your wife. We were sitting on the steps of the University Medical Clinic; the warming sun gave us pleasant shivers. I also remember it was January 21, the year of the Allied landing at Anzio. You said, "Only if you don't mind!" And then, "Why are you laughing?" (I was thinking that "if you don't mind" was the only thing left of the old Ferruccio.)

41

You said, "...Enzina left me because I refused to put my arm around her when we were walking downtown. You know? She came just a little above my elbow and it seemed to me that people would laugh at us like two freaks in a side show. As long as we were on the side streets or in the neighborhoods, I was glad to go arm in arm, but not on the main streets where there were so many people and you never knew who you might meet. Instinctively I would separate from her and talk to her looking straight ahead as though we weren't together. She wanted to go there on purpose to test me, but every time it got worse. I would even walk ahead of her a few steps. Enzina didn't have a sense of the ridiculous. She said that if I was ashamed to be seen with her it meant I didn't love her. But I loved her, and how! She was a healthy girl, clear-headed. And then she was a little girl: she was sixteen years old. She was stubborn and there was no way to make her understand; we fought. One day she said to me: 'Maybe you and I love each other, but it's clear we don't get along. So let's stay good friends and never speak again.' What would it have cost me to take her by the arm downtown? When she said that to me I felt like I could put myself next to her on a stage in the middle of Piazza del Duomo. And yet I said to her, 'Suit yourself.' At home I cried all night. *My father* thought I was dreaming and tried to wake me up. I couldn't stay away from Enzina — every moment I had free I ran to her. She ironically asked my advice about one of our acquaintances who was courting her. I understood that I could still attract her, but less so every day that went by. When I realized that her feelings were truly changing from love to friendship, instead of making a joke of it, I decided to make her jealous! Do you know the piazza a short distance away from the office where I worked? The window of my pigsty looked out on the piazza. There are trees, aren't there, and a fountain in the middle. I often saw a girl leaning on the fountain — she, too, very young. I would look out the window and she would smile at me. She always arrived late in the afternoon. One evening I spoke to her and she walked to the post office with me to mail some things. She continued coming to the piazza; she would saunter about the trees, lean on the fountain, and look at my window. We became engaged, and I ran immediately to tell Enzina about it — I'll never understand why! Enzina changed from day to night in my regard. Instead of making her jealous I lost her completely."

Your roommate, Signor Pepe, called you from the balcony to tell you they were delivering the food. The hospital is like a barracks where you eat at four in the afternoon. You told him, "Let them put it on the dresser. Today my brother is not in a hurry." We moved a little to stay in the sun.

"The new girl was tender and sweet. She seemed like a little kitten and although I didn't love her, I didn't mind being with her. She was tall enough and, seen from far away, we couldn't have made a bad couple. Why are you laughing?"

"Seen from far away!"

"Yes, because up close she wasn't as elegant as Enzina. She didn't take trouble with her hair, even when she went out. But her height was another thing. She was a factory worker, used to working hard and doing without and neglecting herself since she was a little girl. But little by little I understood she wanted more attention. Do you remember that time that you were traveling with your wife, and we four went on a boat? My fiancée was beautiful that day. I remember it very well because it was as though I discovered her only then and realized that she was a woman I could fall in love with. I decided to marry her. It was a decision made coolly and at the same time a kind of insanity. Between the two of us we made sixteen lire a day.... *My father* tried to discourage me in every way he could; he ended by giving me the only furniture he had left, to furnish my house. You, too, tried to convince me not to do anything in a hurry. Do you remember what you said to me?"

"It seems to me like you want to get married to win a bet. But if this anxiety is love, then you are doing the right thing. That is more or less what I told you."

"And I said it was really love...."

You were smiling and looking humiliated at the same time. You asked me for a cigarette. The sun had left us and I wanted you to put my cap on your head, to protect yourself from the temperature change. You said, "Sometimes I could say I married to spite Enzina. But it wouldn't be the truth. The truth is I needed affection. I looked for it in marriage. Little by little, and because of the misery we suffered together, I came to truly love

101

my wife. Our love was more than holding one anothers' hands.... Never to have had anyone I could really be myself with, anyone who understood and gave me courage...."

Your voice trembled; I didn't know what else to do but touch you.

"My father has been a good friend to me but it's no good trying to tell him some things. There's too great an age difference between us. Besides, there are no words to explain oneself. Sometimes a caress is enough. That's it, I've never had that caress.... And my wife has always been closed, *I've never been able to talk to her.* Do you know what I mean when I say talk?"

"I believe so," I answered. Your words made my heart beat faster.

Your hands were crossed on your knees, and you were looking straight ahead. There was a flower bed with a huge tree with stripped bark in the middle. The early evening shadows fell quickly; but the air was still warm and windless. A warm evening at the end of January. Barely a year has passed and I remember those moments as though lived in distant youth, with my brother next to me confiding his pain.

You said, "And now that my little girl can talk I can't enjoy her!"

42

The month of February went by. It was March. The tree with the stripped bark put out leaves, and last spring began. After the illusory improvement you had a relapse. A more intense cure — another mark on the white page of your body — gave you your strength back, but it was, as you said, the beginning of sulfonamide poisoning.

You had become good friends with another patient. He told you about his being an anti-Fascist, being chased by the Fascists, and then jailed for some time, which led to his illness. Upon his return from jail he found his wife living with another man, his two children in an orphanage. He had told you of his own deep feelings for his children and for his wife whom he still loved in spite of everything. He was very ill, and so poor he didn't even own a suit. You shared cigarettes and homesickness. You told me about him, "His situation is similar to mine. I have also abandoned my wife to the world, though under different circumstances and against my will.... How I would have blamed her if...."

Your friend was a cordial and expansive young man. One day he got the idea of going to see his children who were in boarding school. Since he had nothing to wear to go out, you offered to get him the necessary things from the other patients of your same ward. "I want to look good," he told you and slyly suggested what he wanted from each person. The best from each, that is. Number 8 gave him his suit, Number 2 his shirt and tie, Number 13 his socks, and 7 his hat. You gave him your overcoat and your bed neighbor, Signor Pepe, who was to be operated on that day, gave him his shoes. Thus, elegant and touched by emotion, he left the hospital. He was wearing your coat, the only decent thing you possessed, and under which you had hidden your shabby, faded, and patched suit up to that time.

In the evening your friend did not come back, nor the day after, nor the day after that. Number 8, a clerk, had loaned him his only suit. Sick people are egotistical, the black marks burn their flesh, they hate the world like guilty and unrepentant prisoners; any complaint is good for their lamentations. Number 8 reminded you that you were the guarantor, which 22 echoed by calling you an accomplice in a swindle. Number 7 also joined the chorus, and 13 of the socks — an old man suffering from asthma and arthritis who said that all his life he had always regretted any act of generosity. Only Signor Pepe who died under the knife made no show of his feelings.

At first you were hurt. "Perhaps he couldn't stand the excitement of seeing his children again and had a heart attack.... Your accusations are shameful and unjust.... He may be dead and you're insulting the memory of an unfortunate man, politically persecuted...."

The fourth day came and the wife of Number 8 who had vainly pursued her husband's suit from one address to another brought back the news: they were dealing with a common delinquent, several times condemned for theft; neither wife nor children existed, but a mother and a sister to whom he had done "more than the Germans in Poland."

You suffered as though inflicted by an inner blow. Your temperature went up. Number 8, who was only there for observation "for a suspected ulcer," had to leave the hospital and couldn't. His bed was in front of yours and you stayed all day with your head hidden under the covers in order not to meet his gaze. Until his wife found a relative who would loan him a suit. But Number 8 was a tall man and all the ward laughed when he left with the trousers coming only midway down his legs. Before leaving he came to your bed and shook your hand, saying, "Oh, 16! I've got nothing against you! I've got it in for that scoundrel!" A little later you told me, "He looked honest, and he was a jailbird! The most upsetting thing about this is that he pretended to have the feelings that I really have. I've learned from this that there's no dividing line between truth and lies. It's frightening!"

43

The top doctor who had cured Big Head kept marking up your body and took it into the middle of the amphitheater so the medical students could learn how to pursue an unknown illness. He conducted the lesson with the page open to your name. Then, from time to time, he would say to his assistants, "Put a period and begin a new paragraph." Until, from one cancellation after another, your wounded, unusable page was covered with marks. The relatives who asked, with death in their hearts, were told, "The organism no longer reacts!"

Now the top man is no longer involved. It is his assistants who have a free hand. And that hand is a heavy one that leaves deeper marks. They administer doses of a remedy so unnatural that it makes a lesion on your kidneys. They rush to correct it with a transfusion and do it so quickly it causes a serious reaction.... If Joe Lewis were given a sure, clean blow to the jaw, he too would have gone down on his knees, his organism would have no longer reacted, the champion would have begun his ten-seconds' agony. Mortal agony lasts longer than a boxer's who loses his fight, and it is heartrending, cruel, unspeakable.... To relieve you of pain they gave you injections. One day a young, pretty nurse —an innocent —absentmindedly inserted the needle. The next night you complained of pain. The doctor on duty came, examined you, said, "It's nothing! Only an impression!" The impression became an abscess; they cut into you, but your tired flesh, mark after mark, instead of closing back up spread the abscess over your buttocks like leprosy.... They had to bandage you like a newborn. It was a good reason to suspend every medical attention, waiting for it to heal!

(The doctors at this point became Pontius Pilates. "The organism no longer reacts!" And if they were forced to face their responsibility, they sent the nurse to find the doctor on duty!)

44

Now you were immobile in your bed and outside the windows it was the height of spring. The smells reached your bed; you looked at the bit of sky for a long time and said, "What did I do that was bad?" You squeezed my arm as hard as you could, asking me, "Am I hurting you?" "No," and I saw your eyes darken.

"Am I hurting you?"

"No, squeeze, squeeze."

I was thinking that it made you happy to squeeze my arm, as a relief.

"Sure I'm not hurting you?"

"No. Don't worry."

You had a desperate expression, and your eyes filled with tears. "Don't you know I have no strength? If I have no more strength, how can I fight the illness? It's the end. I don't want to die, I want to live another ten or twenty years...."

Only then I understood. "But of course you hurt me. I said no just to be nice."

You flashed me a look of pity, crossed by a shadow of scorn. "Why lie to me?" you said. I pulled up my shirt sleeve to show you the mark of your fingers on my skin. You smiled like a baby, convinced. "I'm sorry," you said. And then, "Give me a kiss." And then, "You're the only one I have, don't leave me." You were affected, frightened by your own words. "Give me another kiss."

There were visitors everywhere on the ward at that evening hour — friends, relatives. "Look," you said to me, "everyone has someone who loves them. They may just come out of a sense of duty, but it's a consolation.... I live night and day for this time when you come. Aren't you at all embarrassed for them to see us kissing? I have such a need for affection.... I've always felt alone. Never so much as now."

One day I found you strangely calm and rested. You seemed to have fallen into a languor. It was toward the end of April, with a great sun outside whose rays were caught by the screen on the balcony. After a long silence you said, "I thought about mama all night and I discovered why I've felt alone all my life. I've missed her. If she had lived,

my whole life would have been different.... You
knew her —what was she like? Do you still have the
photograph with her hair fringed and puffed on the
sides? Do you remember her combing her hair like
that?"

"No. I remember her with her hair pulled back
and hanging loose."

"She had black hair, didn't she? But we were
blond as children, and afterwards became
darker...."

And then, "Is it true that she looked like you?"

"That's what they say."

"She must have been good like you are."

"She really was good. Grandmother used to say
she was a little nervous."

"Perhaps because of her illness."

"What illness?"

"She had the falling sickness, didn't she?"

You said it like that: "falling sickness," and you
looked at me. Your look was sweet and blue and
timorous like you were involuntarily revealing a
truth.

"I'm hearing it from you for the first time!"

Now you seemed surprised, lying there, raised
on your pillows with an almost sulky air. You said,
"Why do you want to hide it from me? What's bad
about it?"

"There's nothing bad about it. It's just not true,
that's all."

"Grandmother even told me it was true."

"That's not possible. But besides...." I understood that my words were a kind of affirmation to
you. I didn't want to tire you.

You said: "Tell me something more."

"What?"

"I don't know. If you are a writer, describe her to me. Tell me something so I can see her in my imagination."

You took my hand in yours, looking at me as though terrified. Your blue eyes were seeking support from me —they were the eyes of a little boy who has lost his mother. You said, "I need her when I'm alone. I need to ask her help. She'll understand when I ask her to pray for my little girl. But I have to think about her alive. When I imagine myself talking to a ghost, I lose courage."

Your bed was the last one in the row, near the balcony. You said, "Fix the screen so we're separated from the others and it'll seem like I want to be alone. Then we can talk about mama."

To console you I would have liked to invent something. But I had fallen into your same anxiety; I was experiencing your agitation. "Calm down," I said to you, and I said the same to myself. "Mama will hear you the same if you pray to her, even if you pray to an abstract image. Tomorrow I'll bring her photograph."

"No," you said. "I want to imagine her alive. As if I had seen her and heard her speak." And then, "If it's true that she resembled you I can imagine her from your face. But how can it be that mama had your face?"

"In fact, it was different."

"How was it, then?"

"I don't know, Ferruccio!"

"Didn't you know her? If you're a writer, describe her to me."

"I don't remember her alive, either. I just remember her on her deathbed."

"How?"

I told you how, roughly, and as I talked to you it was as though I were freeing myself of a secret kept too long inside of me.

"You scare me," you were smiling, apprehensive. "And if I die will you brush a fly away from me?"

Then, childishly, I began to cry. I put my face on your chest so you wouldn't notice. You said: "Get off, you big lug, you're heavy. I don't want to die!"

You said, "Haven't you ever asked our father about mama?"

"Yes, but he didn't tell me anything concrete. One day I asked him purposely about her. When I got back home I wrote down what he said so I would remember."

"Do you still have what you wrote?"

"I think so. If I find it I'll bring it tomorrow."

I found it, and the next day I read you what our father had remembered about our mother.

45

12 September 1938. I went to meet papa at the shop where he worked. I asked him again about mama. A synthesis of our discussion went like this:

I: "How did you meet mama?"

He: "I was a clerk in a paint shop on Via Calzaioli. Mama worked as a dressmaker on the Corso, nearby."

I: "Who introduced you? How did you happen to speak the first time?"

He: "How do you expect me to remember? It's been 27 years!"

I: "When you asked her to be engaged did she say yes immediately?"

He: "I think so. We were engaged for ten months. Her parents made some trouble, but she said if they didn't allow her to marry me she would kill herself. She was capable of doing it."

I: "How do you know she was capable of doing it?"

He: "Just that. You can't give words to some impressions!"

I: "Did she love you a lot?"

He: "Yes, of course. But she was a strange woman. I never understood her very well."

I: "Is there something you don't want to tell me?"

He: "Nothing. Absolutely. She was strange...."

I: "For example?"

He: "What can I tell you? For example: if she decided to go out. She would get all dressed up and everything. Then she would change her mind and want to stay home."

I understood that papa had nothing more to tell me, that for him mama's memory is something distant and general, unreasoned. It intimidated him to speak to me, and I noticed that he pitied me as though I had some mania.

46

Each day your body became more consumed, but it was as though in the slow consumption of your flesh the sensitivity of your soul was refined. Strength of nerve kept you miraculously alive and gave me false hope to which even my reason acquiesced. The abscess was healing, and your mysterious illness, though not yet cured, gave unexpected signs of improvement. But your body was collapsing against itself. When I helped the nurses wash you and change the sheets, your torment made me grit my teeth. A hard cover of parchment seemed to be stretched over your man's skeleton; only your relaxed mass of muscles were sensitive to the touch. The nurses gave you injections between the nerves of your thighs after long, patient exploration. Your beautiful athlete's body had vanished; the hemorrhages and draining from the wounds on your buttocks had gradually dried up. Your pale face, illuminated by the blue flame of your eyes, expressed a vitality that shined with hope, but which at the same time accentuated the tragedy. Settled back in bed again, with only your face and beautiful long hands uncovered, your spirit came back to delude me.

You said, "I've gone down hill, haven't I? But I'll get back on my feet. As long as you don't leave me.... I thought over all you told me about mama's epilepsy. Now that I think about it, it seems to me that grandmother said yes to my question without understanding what it meant."

"Did you call it 'falling sickness'?"

"Yes."

"Then she certainly wouldn't have understood. If you had said convulsions she would have answered no."

"Will you get angry if I ask a question?... Is it true that mama was crazy?"

"It's not true. That's an idea you've had since you were a boy, but it's all a lie."

"I know she died of meningitis as a consequence of complications from delivery, in addition to the flu. But she wasn't crazy before that?"

"No, no, no. They let you think that!"

"No one told me that. *I imagined it by myself.* I have carried the idea inside me. During these nights I spend with my eyes wide open I ask her pardon, and I don't think I ever ask it enough. Now I understand why I try to imagine her alive, because the image I had was that of a crazy woman!"

You were lucid, serene; the nurse had made you a camphor poultice, and your breathing, usually labored, was now easy. You seemed to have come out of convalescence. The orderly began his shout, "Signori, it's time!" A nurse came around the screen where we were hiding and asked you, "Do you need anything?" and went away. We could hear the relatives saying good-bye to the patients, then from the next bed a dialogue between your neighbor and one of his relatives reached our ears. ("Go on home," said the sick man. "Everyone else has gone. If you stay any longer they'll scold me." "Someone over there is hiding behind the screen," the relative said of me. "I'm going to stay as long as he does." And the sick man said: "But he has permission. His brother is very ill, more gone than here!") Your cheeks reddened slightly, with a sudden movement a cry of pain wrenched from you. You struck the screen, shouting, "Stupid! I'm more alive than you!" The screen fell on the shoulders of the visitor, all the ward was in an uproar, the nurses came running. You were lying flat now, exhausted, crying, with your mouth twisted like a baby.

"Everyone thinks that, and you don't want to believe them!" you said between sobs. "You don't love me if you make fun of me like that. You come to talk to me and I am dying.... Go away, go away, I don't want to see you any more. You kid me that I'll get well when you know there's no more hope.... Go away, go away...."

You gradually calmed down. Reaching for my hand, you brought it to your lips with a convulsive motion, bathing me with saliva and tears: "I'm a bad person," you stammered, "but I don't want to die...."

47

May passed in this desperate struggle, in crises and miraculous recoveries. There were days of absolute prostration when your face acquired a lunar pallor, and your wounded lips were like spent craters. "I have a tongue like a cow," you said to me. You spoke with difficulty; I had to watch your face in order to understand your words. Your breathing was slow and harsh and your aquamarine eyes seemed diluted, veiled by a white curtain. Your skin was dry, like a scaly, dried fish to the touch. "I change skin like a snake," you said. "I'm dehydrated and need to drink a lot."

On other days you flourished incredibly. Your eyes recovered their brightness and illuminated everything. You looked at yourself in the mirror; "I'm all eyes and nose," you said. You often had a beard stubble that gave you a convalescent air. Your every word was a desire for life. One day you said to me, "During the crises a voice tries to tell me to close my eyes and let go. It's a sweet sensation that frees me from pain. It's as though I'm about to go to sleep, but I do everything to keep from it. I'm afraid I'll never wake up. Sometimes sleep sneaks up on me; I wake up suddenly, like I had returned to life from death."

Then you said, "I think you die when you are prepared to die. So I've quit taking communion. The priest and sister are annoyed with me, but I realize that when they say they are praying for me to get well they are preparing me for death."

"Do you believe in God?" you asked me.

"Yes."

"Why do you say yes if you don't believe? Do you also want to prepare me for death?"

"Nonsense! It's just that I think it's ridiculous to say, write, or demonstrate non-belief in God. Everyone has to face death. If a man can no longer hope for anything in the world of men, at that time he will be able to do without God. Only then can he say he doesn't believe."

"And if he can't hope in men anymore and can't hope in God, what can he hope in?"

"He can still believe in himself. He recognizes himself in all those he has left behind."

"Then you still hope in men?"

"Yes, I still hope in men if not in God."

"And this is communism?"

"Even this," I said to you.

"Do you remember when we were talking about this a few months ago? It seems like a century ago. Is the boulevard with the trees still outside the gate?"

"Of course it is."

"Will you show me Rome when I get well?..."

Then you said, "After all, God is really an

115

abstraction. Even when I talked to him I could never see him nor imagine him, not even as a light. Instead of thinking of God, I thought of Jesus."

"Did you see Jesus?"

"Yes, Jesus, yes. I always thought of a statue of Jesus taken from the cross that they exhibit during Holy Week in the Chapel of Misericordia."

"God is Jesus."

"Yes, but he was a statue all the same. And when I saw him I always saw the chapel full of people, and I was with the people and Enzina was next to me. I remember particularly one Good Friday when Enzina and I made a tour of the churches.... Now I think of God in another way."

"How?"

"I think of mama. She's surely in Heaven. And it's useless to think about an abstract God, so I think about mama.... It's a shame you didn't find her photograph.... Since I don't want to sleep, I dream with my eyes open. A few nights ago I thought I saw her holding my little girl's hand. They came towards me and my little girl smiled. But mama wasn't smiling. I saw her indistinctly, as though she were surrounded by fog. That's why I asked you to help me imagine her. Sometimes I start thinking about her deliberately. Then I close my eyes and try to make her speak. But I can never hear her voice or see her move. I can't even see what she is wearing. Do you remember how she dressed?"

"I remember what she wore for the last time. A black suit, with a long skirt."

48

I didn't know how you got nourishment. You wanted everything, you tasted nothing. You wanted things that were impossible to have. You complained about my ineptitude if I couldn't get you what you thought would make you happy: early fruit, fresh and light, warm, fragrant. You envied everything the relatives of the other patients brought them. You always wanted something different the next day, and I was never in step with your whims — *never in time to make you happy for an instant.* Then you would hug me and beg my pardon for your harsh words, you would cry.

One day you asked me for orange marmalade. It was a morning at the end of May; I ran through the whole city, from shop to shop, from refusal to refusal. The shopkeepers would shake their heads like I had asked for something absurd, a piece of planet Mars. I perspired from running from street to street, shop to shop, and from one ironic smile after another. Perhaps I had never hated the Germans nor felt the horror of war any more than I did during those hours. Desperation and fraternal selfishness took away my reason: I was a blind, unreasonable man looking for a jar of orange marmalade with the impetuosity of a street bandit, with the peevish voice of a beggar, in vain.

I brought you a small jar of cherry preserves that you tasted and rejected like bile. In the anxiety of the long search I had unpardonably forgotten your dinner! You didn't want to let me go out again. "I don't want to be alone," you said. You disguised your tantrum with sarcasm. You voraciously ate the normal hospital food: too much poison for your wounded organism. You said, "It's not your fault! *If some day I want some grass there won't be a blade left anywhere."*

There was no orange marmalade for you in all of Rome for days and days. Every time I came to your bedside, I would see your look of hope. "That marmalade reminds me of so many things. I see they are all things truly dead and buried!" you said on one of your last days.

49

During this same time you said, "I've been thinking about that page in your diary where you wrote your conversation with our father. After all, he was right. What's important to us about mama isn't important to him. It's logical that he wouldn't remember. I see it with my wife. I don't find anything extraordinary in her either, because she is my equal and something that completes me. I tell you, I want to get well almost more for her than for my little girl, if it were possible to distinguish more and less in this case. What's good for my little girl is a different thing; *in this sense it's the same as what's good for the mama!"*

It seemed like you had seen a marvelous light; your eyes were lit up in happy amazement. You said, "That's why I so often see my little girl hand in hand with mama!" And suddenly you darkened: "That doesn't mean that her life's in danger? Why don't they write me! Telegraph them, please.... Or is it like I thought before: mama holds her hand to show me she is under her protection!"

Your vacillations, depressions, excitements took more and more of your strength. You had to lie still in bed, resentful that your body could never find a comfortable position, weak and hurt as it was. The doctors ordered injections and "medicine for the heart," expecting, with all their science now powerless, for your organism to react. And the other patients, selfish and closed in their own illnesses, which were always less than their neighbors', didn't come near your bed anymore. "They keep their distance as though I had the plague," you said. There was the odor of death around your bed, the smell coming from the abscess. And with the first heat of June the flies, the flies! Circling your head, resting on your face, at the corners of your mouth, at the corner of your eyes as soon as you dozed.

You were dozing off for longer periods; you would open your eyes every time as though coming back to consciousness after a faint. One day you said to me, "Mama came to me while I was sleeping. This time she spoke. She told me to be quiet, that she was thinking of me, to make me well. I saw her very clearly. She was dressed like a girl today, with short sleeves and hair all loose on her shoulders."

Then you had a surprising return of strength — it was the renewal that precedes the agony. You told me, "I want to go away from here. They aren't curing me anymore. I want to go back to Florence while I'm still alive and have hope of getting well. I want to see my little girl and my wife again!"

The doctors calmly agreed. They said, "It could be that the change of air would help him.... At least he'll be able to make the trip...." *At least!* An ambulance came with two solicitous Red Cross nurses. I was to go to Florence by other means.

It was a breezy, warm morning; going down on the stretcher you saw the barkless tree again. "Damn it's green!" you said. But when the stretcher was in the ambulance your pleasant mood vanished. You took my hand, crying, your lips clamped between your teeth. When you opened your mouth for a moment, a white mark was under your nose and on your chin, whiter than the rest of your face, so tight had you gripped your teeth. The blue of your eyes shone through the tears.... Then the ambulance disappeared down the street. Only then did I admit to myself that I hadn't wanted to accompany you so I wouldn't be there when you died. *I wanted to remember you alive.*

50

It was a cruel June, so thick with life, with frantic activity outside the hospital gates. Just beyond the boulevard, at Porta Pia, was a neighborhood amusement park, with an automobile race track, bumper cars, and shooting galleries. The loud speaker blared popular songs. Going away from the hospital, I walked aimlessly here and there in the middle of the clamor, unable to think. That morning of our farewell I found myself before a shop window on Via Salaria where jars of sweet preserves were stacked pyramid fashion. At the top of the pile were jars of orange marmalade. As I looked at them the fruit stamped on the label seemed like a winking face. My ideas and convictions, the love that I had for my wife and for the little girl also born to me, my faith in my work, the truth that my dearest friends had died for in the Resistance, my humanity and my aspirations, all reeled before the injustice of your fate. Now I tell myself that for both the purest and the most corrupt souls, death is merely a normal event of life; it is the completion of understanding. But for souls no longer pure and not yet sinful, that know neither the taste of renunciation nor the pleasure of wickedness? "Blessed are the poor in spirit; for theirs is the Kingdom of Heaven," said Christ. If that is true, your soul shines in the highest heaven.

Naples, December 1945

This Book Was Completed on January 30, 1988
at Italica Press, New York, New York and
Was Set in Galliard. It Was Printed on
55 lb Glatfelter Natural Paper with
a Smyth-Sewn Binding by
McNaughton & Gunn,
Ann Arbor, MI
U. S. A.
* *
*